LIVE YOUR PURPOSE

A THREE-STEP MODEL

DR. KEITH OGLESBY

Published by

Keith Oglesby

Dallas, Texas

Lynchburg, VA

USA

To Book Keith Oglesby for your next event:

Email – koglesby1@liberty.edu

Website - www.liveyourpurpose.org

Design work by Maggie Smith

Printed in the United States of America

ISBN

DEDICATION

This book is dedicated to our Lord and Savior, Jesus Christ.
This researcher acknowledges that we have no original thoughts but
are encouraged to be good stewards of the passion, spiritual gifts,
personality, ideas, testimony, and life experience to meet the needs of
others graciously granted to us by God through His Holy Spirit
(Colossians 1:15).

ACKNOWLEDGMENTS

I want to acknowledge my personal Lord and Savior, Jesus Christ. We have no original thoughts that are not given to us by our Heavenly Father. All of this book's glory, honor, and outcomes belong to Him and Him alone.

I also want to thank all of the leaders who have invested in me in my educational and camp ministry journey, especially the faculty at Liberty University, the Board of Directors at Carolina Creek Christian Camps, and the founders, Dr. L.E. Richey and Shelley Richey, and Rusty and Paula Walter, who have been very influential supporters and mentors in my life.

I want to thank Maggie Smith for "living her purpose" by being willing to use her incredible creative gifts and abilities (spiritual gifts), her heart to serve God and others (passion), and her desire to expand the Kingdom by both modeling and encouraging others (meeting a need) to "chase the light."

I would also like to thank the Altizer family for their amazing support and encouragement (and food) along this journey. I could not have crossed the finish line without you!

Finally, I want to thank my parents, who instilled in me early on that all things are possible with God. I also want to thank my incredible wife, Carrie, for being my soulmate and greatest fan, and my amazing children, Emily, Chris, Josh, and David.

WHAT PEOPLE ARE SAYING

As a pastor, I've never met a person who, at some point in their life, hadn't questioned God's plan for their future. Finding, understanding, and pursuing God's calling and purpose is a difficult task, and there are few resources designed to help us clearly discern God's plan. Until now...Keith Oglesby has developed a terrific resource to help us all ensure God's "next steps" and to live our God-ordained purpose. This book, Live Your Purpose, unpacks a three-step model which will help anyone, no matter their place in life, discover God's will. I highly encourage you to read and implement these principles in order to become all God intended for you to become.

Jonathan Falwell
Pastor, Thomas Road Baptist Church

"I have personally witnessed Keith live his purpose as his co-counselor, a husband and father, and throughout his career as a leader in Christian camping. Working with college student-athletes, I have had hundreds of conversations about majors, graduate schools, jobs, direction, passions, callings, and how to figure it all out. Live Your Purpose will serve as an incredible guide for mentors like me and for those I lead to be able to help discern God's Will for their life. I am fired up to put Keith's model into practice with my guys!"

Chris Creighton
Head Football Coach
Eastern Michigan University

"Keith is a wise, caring, and enthusiastic leader who has invested his life in discipling others. This book outlines a helpful process for guiding emerging adults to follow God's movement and call on their lives. Based on scripture and principles of human development, this is a powerful tool for engaging young people in conversations about vocation, calling, and life purpose. I urge your consideration."

Rob Ribbe, Ph.D.
Executive Director: HoneyRock, Center for Leadership Development
Associate Professor: School of Mission, Ministry, and Leadership - Wheaton College

"When I was in my early 20s, a wise man told me, "find your gifts and build your life around them." That advice served me well, but it did not provide me with handholds to grip that truth and engage it well. Keith Oglesby, in his new book, Live Your Purpose, has provided a practical three-step tool for emerging adults to discover God's pathway for them toward a fulfilling and effective career."

Dan Bolin
Author & President, Refueling in Flight
Former President of Christian Camping International Worldwide
Former Christian Camping and Conference Association Board Chairman

"I have been ministering to campers of all ages and a summer staff of college students for nearly five decades. I can confirm that answering the question, "What is God's will for my life?" is a very common problem for teenagers and college students today. I appreciate how Dr. Oglesby (KO) has spent a long time developing this simple but proven model to help others answer this question based on Biblical principles and a life of proven ministry experience. I highly recommend this book to any student, parent, youth pastor, or camp director helping students who are seeking God's will for their lives. Proud of you, KO! Great job!"

Joe White
CEO – Kanakuk Kamps

"God has uniquely gifted and strategically positioned Keith Oglesby (KO) to impact college students by helping direct them to serve the Lord within their gifting and passions. KO is a godly man, biblically grounded, who genuinely cares for college-aged men and women to find their God-ordained vocation. I've seen firsthand that KO lives out his research as he has mentored my son, Caleb, helping him navigate the Lord's direction in his life, for which I am deeply grateful."

Mike Romberger
President/CEO – Mount Hermon Christian Camp

"This is a rare book! It artfully combines solid research procedures with practical and useful information about a very important topic. I have been guiding dissertation research for almost thirty years, and I can attest to the fact that Dr. Oglesby has done his homework. He grounds his biblical knowledge and decision-making insights in carefully crafted research. While many talk about the integration of faith and learning, this book actually does it, offering spiritual benefits of eternal significance to all who read it and use it."

Stephen D. Lowe, Ph.D. (Michigan State University)
Professor of Christian Education: John W. Rawlings School of Divinity
Liberty University

"KO has lived his life on purpose! Over the last three decades, I have had the privilege of seeing him live out that purpose as a husband, father, friend, camp director, and professor. He passionately pursues Christ and models what it means to know and experience God's will as he shares in this timely book. As this and future generations navigate God's call on their lives, I cannot think of a better guide for them than KO and the lessons he has learned over a lifetime of pursuing and doing the will of God."

Mike Taylor
Vice President of Mobilization
Greater Europe Mission

"Dr. Oglesby (KO) is one of the most respected and skillful leaders I have ever met in any field. The caliber of his experience as a practitioner and researcher is unrivaled. He is humble, persistent, and thorough. I highly recommend anything he has researched and written to my students and their parents and any NexGen leader looking to teach their high school students a model to help them discern God's will for their lives."

Dr. Derik Idol
Professor, Executive Director of Center for Youth Ministries
Liberty University

"One of the most basic questions burning in the hearts of college-age students centers around purpose. Plenty of books and podcasts validate that we have a purpose on this planet, but few unpack how to know what it is... until now. Dr. Keith Oglesby's book *Live Your Purpose* presents a biblical model for finding and fulfilling God's plans for your *life. Not only are the principles grounded in Scripture, but college-age students are hungry for direction in this area. In fact, KO offered to teach the content to my staff of 100 college students. 90% voluntarily showed up with journals in hand... before breakfast! KO is experienced, informed, grounded, and has a message that college-age students want and need to hear!"*

Jon Estes
Director & CEO
Woodlands Camp and Retreat Center

"It is so common for young committed Christians to struggle to know God's will for their lives. Having read Dr. Oglesby's dissertation and new book, Live Your Purpose, I truly believe that the simple model he has created has great potential to help anyone searching for God's will or for those who are mentoring those who are searching."

Bruce Dunning
Author of God of Adventure
Past Executive Director of Medeba Adventure Learning Centre in Canada

"I have heard dozens of summer staff say they will leave Kanakuk and start a camp. Keith Oglesby did it. His story of utilizing proven tactics, combined with his passion and perseverance in chapter fifteen, is both compelling and challenging. I highly recommend his book."

Ward Wiebe
Director of K-West
KANAKUK MINISTRIES

"Dr. Oglesby is an exceptional practitioner, a skilled communicator, an educator, and, as this research shows, a dedicated and gifted researcher. I had the privilege of having Keith, with his wife Carrie, as our Keynote speakers at our National Conference in Australia. They remain standouts, even after several years.

I have been engaged in a vocational ministry for many years where most staff have felt a very strong calling on their lives to this particularly unique ministry. However, having also worked in other sectors, both commercial and for purpose, I know this is not always the case.

Thus, I am excited to see the work Keith has done in developing this tool to assist in guiding a person to discern their particular vocational calling in their lives. We need more people who are gifted, called, and passionate, working where they should be, whether that be as a motor mechanic, an accountant, or a preacher. I pray that as these emerging adults adopt this tool their eyes will be opened, and their thinking becomes clearer as they discern God's purpose for their lives."

Graeme Janes
Chief Executive Officer
Australia Christian Venues Association

"This is a book in which theology and praxis intersect. Many of my students have trouble discerning God's will for their lives, but Dr. Oglesby's model has resonated so strongly with them to such an extent that a year after he presented his model in my class, students are still talking about it. This practical resource should be made available to every Christian student because it offers a concrete method that is easy to understand and life-changing in its impact."

Dr. Mary Lowe
Online Chair and Professor - John W. Rawlings School of Divinity
Liberty University

TABLE OF CONTENTS

HOW TO READ, STUDY, & MAXIMIZE THE EFFECTIVENESS OF THIS BOOK

Thank you again for purchasing this book. I hope this "journey" on the following pages is encouraging, helpful, stimulating, challenging, and fruitful. To get the most out of this book, I encourage you to do the following things *every time* you read it.

P R A Y (1 Thes. 5:17) for God to *speak to you* and reveal *His will* for your life.

R E A D *the following verses every time* you continue to read a new section or chapter to *remind you* that you are created to *Live Your Purpose* (mark this page, so it is easy to find each time you continue your study).

LIVE

Acts 17:28 – "'For in Him we live and move and have our being.' As some of your own poets have said, 'We are his offspring.'"

Philippians 1:6 – "...being confident of this, that He who began a good work in you *will carry it on to completion* until the day of Christ Jesus."

Philippians 1:21 – "For to me, to live is Christ and to die is gain."

James 4:14 – "Why, you do not even know what will happen tomorrow. What is your life? You are a mist that appears for a little while and then vanishes."

Hebrews 9:27 – "Just as people are destined to die once, and after that to face judgment."

YOUR

Psalm 139:13-16 – "¹³ *For you created my inmost being*; you knit me together in my mother's womb. ¹⁴ I praise you because *I am fearfully and wonderfully made*; your works are wonderful, I know that full well. ¹⁵ My frame was not hidden from you when I was made in the secret place, when I was woven together in the depths of the earth. ¹⁶ Your eyes saw my unformed body; *all the days ordained for me were written in your book before one of them came to be.*"

Ephesians 2:10 – "For we are *God's handiwork, created in Christ Jesus* to do good works, which *God prepared in advance for us to do.*"

Jeremiah 1:4-5 "The word of the Lord came to me, saying, "Before I formed you in the womb *I knew you* before you were born I set you apart; *I appointed you as a prophet* to the nations."

Jeremiah 29:11-13 – "For I know *the plans I have for you*," declares the Lord, "plans to prosper you and not to harm you, *plans to give you hope and a future*. Then *you will call on me and come and pray to me*, and I will listen to you. *You will seek me and find me when you seek me with all your heart.*"

PURPOSE

Romans 8:28 – "And we know that in all things God works for the good of those who love him, who have been *called* according to his *purpose.*"

Romans 12:2 – "Do not conform to the pattern of this world, but be transformed by the renewing of your mind. Then you will be able to test and approve what *God's will is—his good, pleasing and perfect will.*"

Ephesians 4:1 – "As a prisoner for the Lord, then, I urge you to live a life *worthy of the calling* you have received."

I Corinthians 9:24-25 – "²⁴ Do you not know that in a race all the runners run, but only one gets the prize? *Run in such a way as to get the prize.* ²⁵ Everyone who competes in the games goes into strict training. They do it to get a crown that will not last, but we do it *to get a crown that will last forever.*"

Mark 8:36 – "What good is it for someone to gain the whole world, yet forfeit their soul?"

2 Timothy 4:7 – "I have fought the good fight, I have *finished the race*, I have kept the faith."

TO RECAP

As you **READ** and **WORK** through this book, I encourage you to answer the questions as you come to them. Take time to pray, reflect, and investigate each element. How has your prayer, Bible study, and consultation with a trusted mentor helped you understand these elements? We spend a lot of time on trivial matters in life. Hopefully, spending time with the Lord and other trusted mentors will provide insight that will benefit you for the rest of your life.

YOU ARE WORTH IT.

PREFACE

THE ROARING RAPIDS

I have spent over twenty-five years in the Christian camping profession designing and building facilities, hiring and training staff, and implementing programming for spiritual development through outdoor adventure experiences. But, to me, it is not merely the *unforgettable* camp experiences (Big Jon Estes, Woodlands Camp) and the rush of emotions from creating these types of breathtaking moments for people, it is also taking the time to "*process*" and participate in "*active reflection*" on these captivating moments.

> "LIFE IS NOT MEASURED BY THE NUMBER OF BREATHS THAT WE TAKE, BUT BY THE MOMENTS THAT TAKE OUR BREATH AWAY."
>
> **TOM IZZO**

In the Christian camping world, I like to say that we creatively and intentionally set up "moments" *with* God that can lead to "movements" *for* God when campers return home to their daily network of relationships.

My good friend, Bruce Dunning, a four-decade veteran of Christian camping and the author of *God of Adventure*, writes that a Christian Adventure is a Bible-based strategy that leaders use to design and guide controlled risk experiences where people are encouraged to say *yes* to God. He then outlines four criteria for Biblical examples of Adventure Leadership:

1. A leader must set up the task or the *experience*
2. The outcome of the experience must be *uncertain*
3. There is *risk* for the participant
4. The experience must be designed for *positive learning*

So, why would I open my book by quoting someone else's? First, because of my love, admiration, and respect for Bruce Dunning. Second, I view the book you are holding as an *experiential learning adventure* that you are about to embark on that meets *all four* of these critical criteria when attempting to discern God's vocational will for your life. Bruce identifies 105 episodes in scripture that meet all four of these criteria in his book.

In this book, my purpose is to design a personal journey between you and God in which you can "*discover*" how he has specifically "*handcrafted*" you for a vocational purpose (from being a Founder and CEO of a Corporation to the next national evangelist like Billy Graham or Nick Hall at Pulse ministries, or even walking in the fruit of the

Spirit (Gal. 5:22) that is required to stay home and minister to your children). I also hope to serve as a "*guide*" for you as you embark on this remarkable road to significance. Let me share an unforgettable outdoor adventure experience from my life in which a *guide* was critical to its success.

In my first year of marriage, my wife and I met friends in Colorado to go hiking and white-water rafting. On our rafting expedition, the first thing that we did was meet our "*guide*." He was friendly, kind, fun-loving, and positive. Like your favorite aunt or uncle. However, as the "newness" of the initial pleasantries and greetings began to wear off, our guide started to use words and phrases like "immediately, when I say NOW, the most dangerous portions of our journey, if you get thrown out of the raft, keep your "nose up" and your "toes up," and if the entire boat FLIPS!!" I can assure you that he suddenly had our undivided attention, and his authority suddenly increased.

He ended his introduction, orientation, and training on the shore by teaching us several commands and the three essential strokes we would need to employ to navigate the river successfully. Finally, he issued a challenge. "This morning, I will assess your ability to learn the strokes and work together as a team. At lunch, we will decide whether or not you have the skill and ability to work together to "attempt" the advanced afternoon portion of the river, which contains mostly level four and five rapids. These rapids can be life-threatening if you do not listen to the guide, act immediately, and have the ability to execute the skills required.

Well, we signed up and paid for the *entire day*, so we collectively determined to show our "*guide*" that we have what it takes to complete the entire journey, no matter what level of danger we face.

I offer you this same challenge right now. This three-step model for discovering God's will for your life WORKS! I have used it for over 25 years and recently completed a scientific study to verify its effectiveness. But, it only works if you learn the three "critical" *strokes* (components), you listen to the *guide* (God), and you obey His *instructions* (commands).

Your *guide* (God and his one and only son, Jesus) designed the *river* (life). He equipped you with *exactly what you need* (passion, spiritual gifts, talents, abilities, testimony, and life experiences) to *navigate* your journey successfully. All of you are in different parts of this journey. Some of you are still in high school, receiving instructions, and about to climb into the boat of making life choices like picking a college, trade school, taking a "gap" year to figure out what you want to do in life, or entering the full-time workforce.

Others are in college now. You are in the boat. You are in the river. But you are struggling to navigate the river. You cannot seem to find your vocational calling. You are not alone, as this book will confirm. In your case, I am going to offer you a practical three-step model (three strokes) to help you discover your calling that has already helped hundreds of students just like you. Or, maybe confirm your calling for others of you. But to use all three strokes, you must listen to the *commands* of your guide (God), who created and designed both *you* and *the river*.

Next, some of you may be parents attempting to help their children, leaders or mentors in ministry, schools, para-church organizations, or camps who need a "training" model to help those you shepherd navigate the river. I hope this model is simple enough for you to teach but profound enough to provide the direction and insight your children and students need to discover God's "good, pleasing, and perfect plan for their lives." *(Rom. 12:2)*

Finally, you may be halfway down the river into your life and career, but you feel trapped, unmotivated, or like you are simply "marking time" from one rapid to the next at your current job or career. Maybe you are searching for a change or significance. You may feel apathetic about your responsibilities, be tired of the same routine, and deeply wish that you were going to work each day with a purpose.

In addition, you could be suffering from anxiety, stress, or physical challenges due to your current employment environment. I have GREAT news. This model works for you, too!

At lunch, when we reached the mid-point of our rafting expedition, our guide took us up to the top of a cliff and showed us the afternoon portion of the rapids on the other side of the mountain. The names of the rapids were daunting, like, "the wall slammer, the boat eater, etc." The mountain view offered a completely different perspective. It was peaceful, beautiful, and refreshing. It was nothing like the roar of the rapids echoing off of the majestic canyon walls towering above us on each side, the splashing of the freezing cold water, and the adrenaline of trying to paddle the right stroke on the correct side of the boat immediately at the command of our guide.

From the mountaintop perspective, we could hear the guide's voice better and see the next stages of our journey. That is my goal for you in this book. At the mountaintop, you can enjoy the view of the mountains and see the course "already" laid out for you (Hebrews 12:1-2). But, make no mistake, after being blessed by this mid-day break and change in perspective, we descended to the river and had to "face" this river, which took courage. It will take courage to trust God and His Word and maybe even step out in faith to pursue His revelations to you in this book. But as the author of Hebrews reminds us, "without faith, it is impossible to please God." The view of the river was refreshing from the mountaintop (God's perspective), but it was intimidating and daunting as we stepped back into the raft.

> IT WILL TAKE COURAGE TO TRUST GOD AND HIS WORD AND MAYBE EVEN STEP OUT IN FAITH TO PURSUE HIS REVELATIONS TO YOU IN THIS BOOK.

I would have never considered navigating this river without a *paddle* (the God-ordained talents and abilities and spiritual gifts (the tools) entrusted to you), *knowledge of the three strokes* (the three-step model in this book designed to help you), and most importantly, the *guide* (God's wisdom, direction, revelation, and Holy Spirit's indwelling to guide you). This book is designed to help you hear from and receive guidance from the One who created you, sent His only Son to redeem you and has a plan for your life! May He guide you in your quest to discover His will, rescue you when turbulence strikes, and welcome you home safely at the end of your life's journey. *So, grab your paddle, climb in the raft, and listen to the guide! Let's embark on this journey of significance together.*

INTRODUCTION

In a recent research project surveying over 1,000 college students, one hundred percent of college students stated that they had been asked by someone, "What do you want to do when you grow up?" Yet, until I published this book, bringing over twenty-five years of ministering to high school and college students, no practical step-by-step model has been developed to help students answer one of life's most important questions from a Biblical perspective.

I hope that the contents of this book, and more importantly, this practical three-step model, will help both individuals searching for God's vocational will for their life and parents, youth pastors, teachers, and guidance counselors, as well as organizations like churches, camps, para-church organizations, high schools, and even universities who are continually asked the question of how one is to discern

"DON'T BE ANYTHING THAT YOU ARE NOT, BUT BE EVERYTHING THAT YOU ARE!"

one's vocational calling for their lives with a very *simple, prayerful, scripture-based, reflective, introspective, and practical three-step model* of how God has created and designed them for a specific vocational purpose.

I often told my summer camp staff at Carolina Creek Christian Camps and now remind my Liberty students, *"Don't be anything that you are not, but be everything that you are!"* Two things happen when you decide not to be anything you are not and to be everything you are. First, you will *not* continually compare yourself to others and feel inferior or jealous because you were not given certain physical features, talents, abilities, or gifts. Second, it gives you the freedom to focus on your *strengths* confidently because you are maximizing your skills and not dwelling on the talents of others.

For example, I love worship music. I have it playing in the background of my life all the time. But I do not have any musical abilities, and I do not covet the fact that Chris Tomlin, Matt Redman, Hillsong United, Elevation Worship, or Maverick City have that ability. I can appreciate and enjoy their giftedness and be grateful that they use their musical gifts and songwriting capabilities to lead me and thousands of others into a deeper relationship with Christ. And as Elevation Worship reminds us, the "Same God" is the giver, healer, and provider of all gifts.

My camp staff and college students will also tell you I am BIG on mission statements. I believe the mission statement is the MOST important principle for individuals, marriages, churches, para-church organizations, businesses, corporations, and Boards. A mission statement should be prayerfully, carefully, and thoughtfully crafted because it should drive and govern all decisions, policies, and resource allocation.

The same is true for you! If you are going to *Live Your Purpose*, you must discover and complete the *mission* that God has entrusted to you. To achieve this lofty but important goal, you must also discern accurately the spiritual gifts and abilities God supernaturally endowed to equip you to accomplish it. It will require you to utilize His anointing, be willing to pursue the proper course of preparation, apply the necessary perspiration, and develop the perseverance needed to be all God has created you to be.

When the Apostle Paul, in First Corinthians and Ephesians, compares the body of Christ to the human body, one body with many distinctive parts, Paul is reminding us all that God's *mission* for us is individualized and His *equipping for our mission is specific* and intentional. I want this book to help you discover this *mission* and utilize all that God has entrusted to you to accomplish it. Then you will bring Him glory (the Chief end of man) and expand the Kingdom by walking in obedience to His calling on your life. When we are not fulfilling our role, we may even be living a life of disobedience and occupying a seat on the bus (Jim Collins, *Good to Great*) where someone else should be sitting. When sitting in a seat that belongs to someone else, we will always struggle to find significance.

PAUL IS REMINDING US ALL THAT GOD'S MISSION FOR US IS INDIVIDUALIZED AND HIS EQUIPPING FOR OUR MISSION IS SPECIFIC AND INTENTIONAL.

This may be you. Maybe you have been trying to discover God's will for your life. Perhaps you are still in high school and have been searching for a few years. Maybe you are in college, and you cannot seem to find a major. Perhaps you are already in the workforce and just unmotivated and unfulfilled. Maybe you are retired and looking to do something meaningful. If you are in any of these categories, I want to encourage you by reminding you of the story of the Chinese bamboo tree.

This particular tree has a seed that is so hard that when planted, it will do nothing for almost five years. Nothing happens in the first year or the second, not the third or the fourth. You must water and care for that seed all those years, seeing no results from your labor. That is, until the fifth year.

In the fifth year, the seed breaks through the soil and grows into a tree. And grow, it does. The Chinese bamboo tree has grown upwards of 3 feet a day, almost 90 feet in about a month. You can literally stand there and watch it shoot up! It has been timed at approximately one inch of growth every 40 minutes.

During those five years, if the person who had planted that seed had stopped watering it or caring for the ground area, the seed would have died. If the planter had gotten tired of waiting and dug up that seed to see what was taking so long or walked away in disgust, the seed would have died. So we can learn that while we have been nurturing and watering the seed of God's vocational will for a long time, I hope that the message, the encouragement, and most importantly, the three-step model presented in this book will provide the breakthrough that you have been seeking faithfully for years. Once you have discovered your plan, I hope you can grow immediately and rapidly into fulfilling God's *mission*.

Finally, research also indicates that many adults feel trapped in jobs they are not necessarily passionate about or gifted in, may have graduated and still be searching, or may be retired and unsure about what lies next. This model is also very successful in assisting these adults in prayerfully navigating and discovering a potential career change to a vocation they are passionate about and gifted in and helping them transition to a more fulfilling vocational pursuit.

One of my former camp directors and early mentors, Bruce Morgan, at Kanakuk and Kids Across America, often challenged us with the phrase, "No Regrets." At the end of each week of camp, he would want us to picture the words "No Regrets" on the back of the sign that hung over the front gate entrance as we walked out of the gate for a rare night off. This simple phrase "No Regrets" would push us to take advantage of every teachable moment throughout the day with our campers. It helped us live more faithfully in our self-discipline in daily prayer and Bible study. It helped us invest more, dig deeper, study more diligently, and serve others more faithfully. I have this same desire for you to *Live Your Purpose* and, at the end of your life, to have "No Regrets."

In the following pages, I will reveal a model that has been highly effective in helping many people discover their God-ordained vocational will. Although ambitious, I have also attempted to include a balance of both "theory" and "application." I desire that this book would please the academic community by the level of research, analysis, and conclusions but also be written so that "lay people" and high school and college students can still benefit greatly and apply it to their lives. The three essential elements of this model are *passion, spiritual gift, and need.* These three vital characteristics are similar to mixing concrete to help you build a solid vocational foundation. *Passion* is like the sand and pea gravel mixture. Without sand and pea gravel, you do *not* have all the "raw" materials needed to create concrete because these two ingredients are critical to forming concrete. Likewise, *passion* is a vital element in the model we will discuss.

Your *spiritual gifting* is like the cement powder. Many people have a passion, but they are missing the necessary hardening agent for the raw materials to solidify into a sturdy and solid foundation. Therefore, they are simply making mud pies by stirring this sand and pea gravel without the key ingredient that gives it the ability to serve its true purpose –to be a solid step, sidewalk, or building foundation.

Finally, understanding how to identify and serve an area of *internal need* within each person and *external need* by being a part of the solution to a problem, a people group, a geographic region, or a cause is like the water which "activates" the sand, pea gravel, and cement mix to properly "bind" together and transform into an entirely new "concentrate" material. Without the water, the dry pea gravel, sand, and cement will merely stay in the wheel barrel or delivery truck but never achieve the purpose of the cement.

Likewise, without the living water and understanding God's purpose, we will never find the vocation, job, and calling that He has entrusted to us to bring Him glory while we are here on earth, live at peace with ourselves and others, or help others realize this same peace and hope of glory and that we will be held accountable for when our brief existence here on earth is over.

We are a vapor, a mist, here today and gone tomorrow (James 4:14). Once cement is properly mixed and hardened over time, you can no longer remove just one of the three critical ingredients from this brand-new concrete. I hope the same permanent transformation takes place for you. I pray the following pages will serve as a guide to helping you discover your true Biblical vocational calling and build a solid foundation for your life. *Let's start mixing!*

> "OUR GREATEST FEAR SHOULD NOT BE OF FAILURE BUT OF SUCCEEDING AT THINGS IN LIFE THAT DON'T REALLY MATTER."
>
> **FRANCIS CHAN**

SECTION ONE

THE HISTORY OF VOCATIONAL CALLING

Most people struggle to determine God's vocational will for their life. One of the primary reasons people have trouble discovering God's vocational will for their lives is that they have no practical model to step them through this process. Most personal and professional growth and development areas have a proven step-by-step method. However, discerning God's professional will for one's life, a question everyone wrestles with, does not.

Hopefully, this book and this new model will encourage you and shed some light (from the Father of lights) on this critical life question. In the Bible, "enlighten" means to illuminate, shine, brighten, or lighten. Strong's Concordance defines "enlighten" as "to cause something to exist and thus come to light and become clear to all." (Luke 11:36, John 1:0, 1 Cor. 4:5, Eph. 1:18, 3:9, Heb. 6:4, 10:32, Rev. 18:1, 21:23, 22:5) The root of enlighten is "photizo." This is where we get the English word "photograph." We add focused light to something invisible, and it makes it visible. I hope that this new model will "shine focused light" on this question of vocational calling which seems invisible to many people, and "enlighten" you to see what God already sees (it already exists) and give you a "picture" of your future.

In addition, when people seek the advice and counsel of trusted adults and mentors to help them determine their vocational calling, which this author highly recommends, these Christian leaders often only have their own life experiences or the life experiences of others to reference. They have no step-by-step Biblical model to assist or recommend to those they lead.

So whether this enlightenment is for the one searching for God's vocational will or those in leadership and mentorship positions of influence in these young people's lives, all people can benefit from this practical step-by-step model to assist them. Unfortunately, until now, this type of model did not exist. Before we examine this new model, the following introductory chapters will provide a brief overview of the historical, theological, theoretical, and sociological perspectives of determining one's vocational calling. May it shed "light" on this subject for you!

CHAPTER ONE
Three Scenarios

scenario one
high school-aged student

KO, "Can I please ask you a question?"

"Sure"

"Well, I am trying to pick a college, but I have no idea what I want to do when I grow up. My parents are putting a lot of pressure to decide where I want to go, but I don't know how to choose a college because I have no idea what I want to major in, where I want to go, or how I should make this decision. Can you please help me?"

"I am not sure, but I would love to try to help. Let me ask you a few questions.

First, what would you do with your life if you had unlimited time to serve people or solve a problem, and money was not a factor?"

"I have no idea. I have never even thought about it like that."

"Okay. No problem. *You are not alone.* I always talk to teenagers who do not know the answer to that question. Let me ask you another question: Do you like to finish a task like a big homework assignment, a project, mowing a yard, painting a fence, or building something, or do you enjoy working with people like having coffee with a friend and listening to their problems and offering advice, tutoring elementary-aged kids after school with their homework, or serving others at your church?"

"Well, I'm not sure. I could enjoy either, but I have never thought about it."

"Okay, let me ask you one final question. If you could solve any problem that is present in our world, or be a part of a team that was working on a solution to a problem like providing healthcare to the sick and injured, placing foster children into potential adoptive families, working in the criminal justice system, providing work for employees to support their families, addressing poverty in the inner city, providing clean drinking water to third world countries, serving on a response team to emergency efforts after a natural disaster, or serving on a research team trying to find a cure for a terminal illness, what type of problem or need in our world would like to try to be a part of the solution?"

"Wow. I am not sure. Do you think I could really be a part of solving a world problem or meeting some local or global need? That sounds amazing. I have never thought about spending my life working in a profession that meets the needs of others. But what would I do? How would I know what needs are out there or how I could help?"

DID YOU KNOW?

Galotti and Mark (1994) note that a significant determining factor in helping students decide what they want to become when they grow up is determined by the college or university they attend (influenced heavily by a faculty member, their peers, and their peer social circles). Galotti and Mark (1994) further note that the college or university a student decides to attend is usually determined during one's junior or senior year in high school.

In the United States, over two million students, their families, and relevant school personnel confront this time-consuming and expensive decision each year, spending over 50 hours investigating information (exclusive of campus visits) and approximately $1,500 indirect costs of preparing materials and gathering information (Litten, 1982). The collegiate choice has long-term ramifications for family ties, friendships, spouse decisions, need for loans, the probability of admission to graduate or professional school, social status, and vocational career paths (Boyer, 1987; Fischer et al., 1987, Litten, 1991). No method or model for discerning God's will is available to help families make this important choice.

scenario two
college-aged student

Dr. Oglesby, "Can I please ask you a question?"

"Sure, what's up?"

"Well, my father is a very successful loan officer at a bank, and my mom is a charge nurse in an emergency room. They want me to major in business or the healthcare industry. But I have taken introductory business classes, and they did not interest me at all, and I cannot imagine being trapped in a cubical from nine to five every day. Furthermore, I am not good when I see blood or people in pain, sick, or suffering. I want to be a teacher, a social worker, or in youth ministry. But, my parents said they would not pay for my school if I majored in one of those fields. I love my parents and want to honor their request, but I am struggling."

"What do you think I should do?"

DID YOU KNOW?

After this exhausting process of choosing a college, research also indicates that since high school seniors and first-year college students do not have an effective method for discerning God's vocational will, an estimated 20 to 50 percent of students enter college as "undecided" majors (Gordon, 1995) and an estimated 75 percent of students change their major at least once before graduation (Astin & Panos, 1969; Theophilides et al., 1984; Kramer et al., 1994). Students who change their college majors are referred to as "major changers" in the education literature. The frequency of a student changing their college major costs both *time* and *money* – additional *time* in school for the student and more *money* for the parents in paying tuition longer.

St. John (2000) perhaps summarizes the process of choosing a major best, "there is, perhaps, no college decision that is more thought-provoking, gut-wrenching, and rest-of-your life oriented-or disoriented-than the choice of a major (St. John, 2000, p. 22).

scenario three
a middle-aged adult

Dr. Oglesby, "Can I please ask you a question?"

"Absolutely."

"Well, I wanted to..... go to law school, so I majored in history or government, ...go to medical school, so I was pre-med, ...travel the world, so I majored in international business, etc., but I did not get into law school, medical school, etc., and I could not find a job traveling in international business. I had to start paying back my student loans, so I got a job to pay my bills while looking for what was next. That was fifteen or twenty years ago. I got married, we had kids, and I had to work, but I am so unsatisfied with my job. I am unmotivated to go every single day. In addition, the stress is, at times, unbearable. I have headaches, trouble sleeping at night, and I am so irritable with my spouse and children. I feel trapped, but I have to work."

"What do you think I should do? Do you have any advice?"

DID YOU KNOW?

Roese and Summerville (2005) cite meta-analytical evidence that Americans' most frequently *identified life regret is choosing their college major.* Perhaps this regret is because many working adults are currently performing jobs they do not enjoy and merely paying their bills because they had no exposure to a practical and systematic plan for discovering God's individual vocational plan for their lives. Hill and Miller (1981) write that many middle-aged Americans, ages 35 to 50, are currently working in a job that they are *unsatisfied with, feel trapped, have no passion for, or just marking time.* Schein (1978) states, "what is, from the point of view of the organization, simply "turnover" may be, from the point of view of the individual, a major transition crisis involving a search for one's occupational niche" (Schein, 1978, p. 172).

CONCLUSION

I have had hundreds of conversations in my twenty-five years working with high school and college students with individuals represented in these three scenarios. So, a little over ten years ago, I started a quest to find an *accurate* theological, theoretical, historical, and societal answer to help *others answer this critical life question* that everyone faces, *"What is God's vocational will for my life?"*

While research shows that everyone has been asked this question, before this book that you are holding, there has been *no theological and practical step-by-step strategy, method, or model to help people answer this vital question from a Biblical perspective.* So, I dedicated my entire four-year doctoral study to researching and writing my dissertation on how to assist others in answering this fundamental life question. This book summarizes my research findings and offers a practical three-step model to help high school students choose a college, college students select a major, and middle-aged adults who feel trapped in an unfulfilling career identify a more significant and life-giving vocational choice.

I pray that this research and new model will assist teachers, counselors, college and university career centers, youth pastors, camp directors, and parents in shepherding those under their leadership with a practical model as a tool to help others discover God's vocational will for their lives and to reach their full potential.

ENJOY YOUR JOURNEY TO SIGNIFICANCE

CHAPTER TWO

The Historical and Theological Perspective of Calling

HISTORICAL PERSPECTIVE

One of life's most challenging questions for teenagers and college students is, "What am I supposed to do with my life?" Many parents, teachers, school guidance counselors, and even ministers attempt to answer this question. Most people answer this question based on their lives or by pointing out successful leaders in various professions. However, merely looking at the success of others does not tell the entire story or the steps of how these leaders successfully navigated the journey to arrive at their current vocational destination (Duffy & Dik, 2013).

While these parents and leaders desire to assist their children and students, most of them do not have a helpful tool, instrument, or model to help them discover the answer to this question from a biblical perspective (Dobrow & Tosti-Kharas, 2011; Elangovan et al.,

2010; Hagmaier & Abele, 2012; Hall & Chandler, 2005). What if an in-depth biblical investigation and a comprehensive review of the precedent literature into how leaders successfully discovered God's vocational will could be created and common themes could be identified? Then, what if a model could be formulated into a universal tool or instrument that could help students find God's vocational will and purpose for their lives? This author believes that if churches, camps, youth groups, para-church organizations, high schools, and Christian universities had this model, they could help people discover their God-ordained biblical vocational calling for their lives. This discovery is what I call *God's vocational will*. My exhaustive journey through the precedent literature and thorough investigation revealed that no biblically-based model exists currently for discovering God's vocational will.

My desire and the proposed model is not for you to discover who you are supposed to marry, what city you are supposed to live in, or even what church you are supposed to attend, but more specifically to discover how God specifically ordained, created, wired, and designed you to serve a vocational purpose with your life.
Biblically, Moses was called to lead the Israelites out of captivity, Nehemiah was called to rebuild the wall, and Paul was called to be the Apostle to the Gentiles. Likewise, Billy Graham was called to the ministry of evangelism, James Dobson to minister to families, and

Wendy Kopp to address the need for teachers in urban communities in America. These are just a few examples of dynamic leaders who followed God's ordained Biblical vocational calling with their lives. When you discover God's vocational will for your life, you will serve with passion, perform a duty that never feels like work, and be internally satisfied because you are meeting a need in this world. The goal of this model, and this book, is to help you do the same.

The concept of career calling has a long history in Western culture. Early conceptualizations considered it a specific request from God for someone to fulfill a particular task or role (Colozzi & Colozzi, 2000). Later, the construct was secularized and modified to emphasize an active search for personal and professional development (Hall & Chandler, 2005; Weiss et al., 2004).

> WHEN YOU DISCOVER GOD'S VOCATIONAL WILL FOR YOUR LIFE, YOU WILL SERVE WITH PASSION, PERFORM A DUTY THAT NEVER FEELS LIKE WORK, AND BE INTERNALLY SATISFIED BECAUSE YOU ARE MEETING A NEED IN THIS WORLD.

Today, religious callings generally refer to missions to serve others (Dalton, 2001; Hernandez et al., 2011); whereas other traditional, non-secular definitions stress that a calling can arise from any identifiable, external source (e.g., God, family legacy) or come from an unknown "push" to the "right place" (Bunderson & Thomson, 2009). Most of these perspectives agree that callings are prosocial and altruistic (e.g., Dik & Duffy, 2009; Hunter, Dik, & Banning, 2010), depict a sense of meaningfulness and mission (Dik & Duffy, 2009), involve matching with and utilizing one's gifts, interests, talents, and opportunities, including drawing on socially significant values and goals and result in enhanced eudemonic well-being (Bunderson & Thompson, 2009; Hagmaier & Abele, 2012; Hardy, 1990; Hunter et al., 2010; Steger et al., 2010).

THEOLOGICAL PERSPECTIVE

Three important things happen when you discover your true God-ordained vocational calling. First, people who successfully discover God's vocational will for their lives will be fulfilling the Great Commission,

> "Then the eleven disciples went to Galilee, to the mountain where Jesus had told them to go. When they saw him, they worshiped him; but some doubted. Then Jesus came to them and said, 'All authority in heaven and on earth has been given to me. Therefore go and make disciples of all nations, baptizing them in the name of the Father and of the Son and of the Holy Spirit, and teaching them to obey everything I have commanded you. And surely I am with you always, to the very end of the age.'" (Matthew 28:16-20)

"And the number of people being added to the community of believers will be expanding daily, Praising God and enjoying the favor of all the people. And the Lord added to their number daily those who were being saved." (Acts 2:47)

> THIS GROUP CONCLUDED THE CHIEF END OF MAN IS "TO GLORIFY GOD, AND ENJOY HIM FOREVER"

Personal and corporate revival can also occur because people will understand how to walk in obedience to their biblical vocational calling.

LIFE QUESTION: WHY AM I HERE?

Why did God create humans in His image, and for what purpose? The Westminster Shorter Catechism was written over five years by one hundred and twenty theologians, thirty laypeople from England, and five commissioners from Scotland who convened in 1643 under the order of the British Parliament at Westminster Abbey. According to this assembly, Boyd (1859) writes that this group concluded the chief end of man is "*to glorify God, and enjoy him forever*" (p.19). Boyd then outlines the *four foundational biblical truths* this group of the brightest and most well-respected scholars of this era formulated to support this conclusion.

First, the chief design of man's creation, in reference to God, was to spread abroad His glory actively. Boyd (1859) cites 1 Corinthians 10:31, "Whether therefore ye eat or drink; whatever ye do, do all to the glory of God..." (*King James Bible*, 1769/2017, 1 Corinthians 10:31) as the primary scripture supporting this claim.

Second, Boyd writes that the chief design of man's creation, in reference to himself, was the enjoyment of God, as noted in Deuteronomy 12:18, "Thou shalt rejoice before the Lord thy God in all that thou puttest thine hands unto" (*King James Bible*, 1769/2017, Deuteronomy 12:18).

Third, the foundation and end of every duty should be the glory of God. Boyd (1859) refers to Romans 14:8 as the critical verse substantiating this element, "Whether we live, we live unto the Lord; and whether we die, we die unto the Lord; whether we live therefore, or die, we are the Lord's" (*King James Bible*, 1769/2017, Romans 14:8).

Finally, Boyd writes that all happiness here and hereafter must be derived from the enjoyment of God as written in Psalms 73:25-26, "Whom have I in heaven but thee. And there is none upon earth that I desire besides thee. My flesh and my heart faileth: but God is the strength of my heart and my portion forever." (*King James Bible*, 1769/2017, Psalms 73:25-26)

According to Boyd (1859), there are *five lessons* that all believers can learn from God's chief *purpose* of creating humans.

1) Humans must make it their **daily aim to honor God**, secure His favor, and seek happiness.
2) Humans' greatest pleasure is *not to be found in this world* but in the *everlasting ages of the next*.
3) Humans have *no right* to make *gaining worldly goods* their *chief desire* and labor.
4) Most humans *mistake* the true business and proper use of this *short life* since they take no proper pains to *honor God* or secure his favor.
5) It must be a *sad and fearful* event to die before one has begun to *live for God and eternity* (Boyd, 1859).

This researcher believes that if this gathering of scholars in the late 1600s concluded that glorifying God and enjoying Him forever was humanity's chief purpose in life, then you must be able to discern God's vocational will for your life to "*glorify Him and enjoy Him forever*." A life spent floundering in the chaotic culture, being tossed (James 1:6) from job to job or city to city, is a life of mediocrity and apathy. It is not only unhealthy mentally and physically, but it is also *disobedient* to the God who *handcrafted you* (Psalms 139:16-19, Ephesians 2:10) and *entrusted gifts to you* (Ephesians 4:1-12) for His

Kingdom purposes while you are **His ambassador** (2 Corinthians 5:20, Ephesians 6:20) here on earth.

Second, people who successfully discover God's will for their lives are more fulfilled because they are using their spiritual gift by doing something that they are passionate about, and they will be meeting the needs of those around them. The three components of *passion, spiritual gifts, and the ability to perform a needs assessment*, the three steps in the proposed model, will be outlined extensively in the following chapters.

Finally, people who struggle vocationally often feel stress, anxiety, feel unfulfilled, and often suffer from burnout (Scott, 2020, para.1). Since this model has been taught to several populations over the last ten years and was validated again in the recent study of over 1,000 college students, perhaps it will help people understand why they struggle with various negative issues in their lives derived from vocations in which they are apathetic. These issues include physical, mental, emotional, and spiritual health issues, including but not limited to stress, cardiovascular disease, migraines, various alcohol and drug addictions, eating disorders, anxiety, and depression (Duffy et al., 2011).

OUR SPIRITUAL IDENTITY: WE WERE CALLED TO "BE" BEFORE WE WERE CALLED TO "BECOME"

According to Small (2018), the image of God is first introduced to us scripturally in Genesis 1:26-27. Small points out that people mistakenly think of an image as a *physical likeness*. However, in this passage, the image of God has historically been considered from two aspects:

> 1) a *functional* view - the authority to rule over the earth, dominion, and
>
> 2) a *relational* view – male and female, be fruitful and multiply.

Small (2018) concludes, however, that there are *three dominant* views of *the image of God:* 1) functional (dominion), 2) relational (male and female), from the Genesis 1:26-27 text, and 3) *substantive view – a non-physical view of the image which cannot be lost.* This third vantage point is *critical* because it claims that *everyone is created by God and in the image of God.*

The *substantive view* gives all people tremendous value and worth. This also means that when people make mistakes, *their image of God cannot be lost,* just their relationship and fellowship with God are interrupted. These people still have tremendous value, which should encourage Christian leaders to reach out to all people in need regardless of their current challenges or personal situation. Small

(2018) concludes that the image of God is not merely a Genesis question. That God continues to develop the concept of the image of God throughout scripture, and that the *image of God is most clearly seen in Jesus.* (John 10:30)

Kilner (2015) reminds us that when it comes to the image of God,-both humanity and Christ have a special connection with God. He writes, "That presently (Christ) and ultimately (Humanity) is a reflection of God" (Kilner, 2015, p. 59). God intends for people to become the "likeness" of God eventually. In contrast, Christ was the exact "imprint" of God, as the writer of Hebrews reminds us,

The Son is the radiance of God's glory and the exact representation of his being, sustaining all things by His powerful word. After he had provided purification for sins, he sat down at the right hand of the Majesty in heaven. (Hebrews 1:3)

This was not a physical likeness but a genuinely holistic and comprehensive creation in His image of our complete physical, mental, emotional, and spiritual being. God's creative process in the garden that day included our *physical characteristics, our mental and intellectual faculties, our emotional stability, and our spiritual awareness* - including the ability to respond to Him when He calls us to salvation by divine revelation of Himself, which leads to our testimony that is to be used for His glory.

THE BENEFITS OF DISCOVERING YOUR VOCATIONAL CALLING

THE BENEFITS OF KNOWING GOD

To walk in God's ordained vocational calling, you must first know God. MacArthur (2012) writes that God's will, first and foremost, is that all people enter into a relationship with Him. MacArthur says the first step for anyone discerning God's will is for them to be saved. He supports this claim in 2 Peter 3:9, that it is God's will "not wishing for any to perish but for all to come to repentance" (2 Peter 3:9).

MacArthur (2012) states that the Apostle Paul reaffirms God's will for all people to come to know him in 1 Timothy 2:3-4, "This is good and acceptable in the sight of God our Savior, who desires all men to be saved and to come to the knowledge of the truth" (1 Timothy 2:3-4). MacArthur (2012) concludes his assessment that discerning God's will for your life begins with salvation when he writes:

> If you are stumbling around in life and tossing up some periodic prayers to God but have never come on your knees to the foot of the cross and met Jesus Christ, then you are not even in the beginning of God's will. God has no reason to reveal to you anything particular about your life because you have not met qualification number one: salvation. (p. 13)

According to Stanley (2010), to fully grasp God's will for your life, you must first understand God's *nature and character*. In the Bible, Genesis tells us that:

> TO FULLY GRASP GOD'S WILL FOR YOUR LIFE, YOU MUST FIRST UNDERSTAND GOD'S NATURE AND CHARACTER.

In the beginning, God created the heavens and the earth. Now the earth was formless and empty, darkness was over the surface of the deep, and the Spirit of God was hovering over the waters. (Genesis 1:1-2)

Therefore, from the beginning of time, *God has always existed.* The word Genesis means "beginning." The remainder of chapter one in Genesis outlines the systematic creation of all living things. Thrasher (2001) writes that "in Genesis, God makes it clear that when He created the universe that we live in, the crowning accomplishment was to create man in his image" (p. 18). Thrasher (2001) further states that we understand the importance of humanity to God from the positionality of the creation of humans in the divine order of creation in Genesis 1:26-27:

Then God said, "Let us make mankind in our image, in our likeness, so that they may rule over the fish in the sea and the birds in the sky, over the livestock and all the wild animals, and over all the creatures that move along the ground." So God created mankind in his own image, in the image of God, he created them; male and female, He created them. (Genesis 1:26-27)

Thrasher (2001) concludes that we can glean two critical things from this reality.

1) These verses remind us that there were (and are) no other gods like the Creator in the beginning, thus declaring His uniqueness.

2) He made man with special care and design, apart from everything else, to enjoy Him in all His perfection.

God designed mankind to *walk, talk, think, and play together*. It may be hard to imagine going for a walk in the park with God, but that is precisely what Adam and Eve enjoyed.

From these two short Bible verses, you can gain several major foundational theological concepts about discerning God's vocational will for your life.

First, humans were created in the image of God. No other animals, planets, stars, or items in nature - ocean, mountain, rainforest, cliff, river, or canyon, can make that claim.

Second, many modern scientists falsely believe that humans evolved from these created things God has given humans dominion over (Hanegraaff, 2001). However, for this book, I will not delve into the various arguments on each side of the debate of creation versus evolution but merely state factually that no scientist had been able to "regenerate" any form of life from "nothing" as God did on this day, today there is no *new* microscopic genetic material being added or created in the universe, scientist, despite trying, cannot "spontaneously generate" a sustainable and regenerate life form from nothing, and there are no transitional fossils between life forms discovered. (Hanegraaff, 2001).

A **third** theological fact in these two verses is that God created them, male and female. In an age when gender identity is highly controversial and debated, one can always go back to the beginning when the Creator of life created all of life. Bird (1981) offers a very comprehensive article articulating the significance of God, creating humans as both male and female. Bird writes that in the history of biblical interpretation and dogmatic speculation, Genesis 1:26-28 has proved remarkably fecund as a source of exegetical and theological reflection. The literature on the passage is now boundless but shows no sign of ceasing or abating, despite the appearance in recent decades of several exhaustive treatments of the text and the existence of substantial consensus among biblical scholars.

WHAT HAPPENED TO GOD'S PERFECT CREATION? WHAT DID GOD DO ABOUT IT?

To discern God's individual vocational will for one's life, one must first enter a relationship with God by believing in His one and only Son, Jesus' virgin **birth, life, death, burial, resurrection, and ascension**, thus receiving the free gift of salvation. This free gift (Ephesians 2:8-9) is available to everyone when they recognize that only one true God created the heavens and the earth. This incredible creation story is outlined in the bible in Genesis, chapter one. The crowning achievement of God's creation was humans made in His image (Genesis 1:27) (Kilner, 2015).

However, this community and intimacy between God and Adam and Eve were short-lived because God told them not to eat from the tree of the knowledge of good and evil (Genesis 2:9). However, God created humans with "free will" to decide for themselves whether to obey His commands or not. In Genesis chapter three, Satan tempted Eve to disobey God's command. She then ate fruit from this forbidden tree and shared the fruit with Adam. From the time Eve and Adam disobeyed God's command, sin and separation from God for all of humanity entered the world.

But, because God is omniscient (all-knowing), God knew that Adam and Eve would disobey His command. Therefore, even in the Garden of Eden, God knew that Adam and Eve would disobey His command and planned to remedy the situation. Four thousand years later, at His appointed time, God sent His one and only Son, Jesus, to earth (John 3:16). Jesus performed many miracles and taught many parables, but his ultimate *mission* was to die on the cross (Romans 5:8, Luke 19:10) to forgive this original sin committed by Adam and Eve and passed down to *all* generations. (Romans 3:23, 6:23, 5:8, 10:9-10).

> JESUS PERFORMED MANY MIRACLES AND TAUGHT MANY PARABLES, BUT HIS ULTIMATE MISSION WAS TO DIE ON THE CROSS, AND RISE AGAIN.

But Jesus did not merely die on the cross. Three days later, *He rose again*! He appeared to the women at the tomb (Matthew 28:9-10), the men on the road to Emmaus (Luke 24:13-35), the disciples on the shore of Galilee (John 21), and twice in the upper room (once without Thomas, once with Thomas, John 20:19-29), and to crowds for the next forty days. He eventually led the crowd to the Mount of Olives and issued them the Great Commission, "Therefore, go and make disciples of all nations, baptizing them in the name of the Father, and of the Son, and the Holy Spirit" (Matthew 28:19). Then He ascended back to heaven (Acts 1:9-11). Finally, he has promised his return like a bridegroom to retrieve His bride, the church (Revelation 21:1-9), and establish a New Heaven and a New Earth (Revelation 21:1).

BELIEVING THAT GOD HAS A PLAN FOR YOUR LIFE

In addition to knowing God, one must also believe that God has a plan for one's life. Sullivan (2016) writes that in the Bible, the Psalmist writes that God created human life, knew everyone before they were even born, and had a God-ordained plan for their lives when he writes:

> For You created my inmost being; you knit me together in my mother's womb. I praise you because I am fearfully and wonderfully made; your works are wonderful, I know that full well. My frame was not hidden from you when I was made in the secret place when I was woven together in the depths of the earth. Your eyes saw my unformed body; all the days ordained for me were written in your book before one of them came to be. (Psalm 139:13-16)

"The Psalmist writes that not only are humans created in the image of God, but that God knew each human before they were even born and that all of one's days were ordained, planned, written, and orchestrated before one was even born" (Sullivan, 2016, p. 25).

In Colossians, the Apostle Paul reminds his readers that God created humans by writing to us:

> The Son is the image of the invisible God, the firstborn over all creation. For in Him, all things were created: things in heaven and on earth, visible and invisible, whether thrones or powers or rulers or authorities; all things have been created through him and for him. He is before all things, and in him, all things hold together. (Colossians 1:15-17)

House (1992) writes that Christ is "the firstborn of all creation" does not mean that Christ is a created being, the first part of all that was created by God in the beginning. "This view of the Arians and more recently of the Jehovah's Witnesses is heretical when the title is seen in its context, particularly in the light of verse 16" (p. 181). House writes that firstborn suggests *supremacy*, not temporality. For example, Israel was designated as God's firstborn in Exodus 4:22, yet many other nations existed before Israel became a nation. God chose Israel to be supreme over all nations as His specially chosen people. House (1992) also writes that in Colossians 1:16, Paul unfolds the meaning of Christ's role in creation:

> "For in Him all things were created that are in heaven and on earth, visible and invisible, whether thrones or dominions or principalities or powers. All things were created through Him and for Him" (Colossians 1:16)

The prepositional phrase in Him may be either a locative-of-sphere phrase (dative of location) or an instrumental phrase (dative of agency). If the former is intended, the phrase emphasizes that creation is centered in Christ. "In the latter meaning, Christ is the direct agent of creation, all things were created by Him" (House, 1992, p. 183). House (1992) maintains that several factors suggest that the first view is preferable.

First, Paul regularly used the words "in Christ" (76 times) or "in Him" (20 times) to indicate that Christ is the embodiment of reality, whether of creation or the redemption of humanity.

Second, the latter portion of Colossians 1:16 refers to Christ as the agency, though indirect, of all creation, "all things were created through Him" (House, 1992, p. 187). Having the idea of agency stated twice in the same verse would seem redundant.

Third, when the instrumental case indicates agency, it usually does not have the preposition ἐν. This preposition, more naturally though not invariably, is locative in meaning (Robertson, 1934). Moule (1953) believes that personal agency is more often expressed in Greek with ὑπο and the genitive. The phrase "in Him" carries more emphasis than through Him. In His role as Creator, Christ was the source from whom all came into being and in whom all creation is contained.

Therefore, humans can be encouraged that if God created all things, this list includes humans – *in His image and according to His plan.* In Ephesians 2:10, Paul would write this in another way,

> For we are God's workmanship, or handiwork, created in Christ Jesus to do good works, which God prepared in advance for us to do. (Ephesians 2:10)

Once again, Paul writes that humans are created in Christ Jesus to do good works, which He prepared in advance." Paul, previously Saul, understood the power of God's redemption and transformation and what it means to walk in the calling God ordained. Paul's three missionary journeys, thirteen letters, and a list of persecutions detail Paul's life of obedience and calling after his radical transformational meeting with Jesus on the road to Damascus (Acts 9).

Finally, Sisson (1986) writes that Jeremiah, an Old Testament prophet in the Bible, writes in his book:

> For I know the plans I have for you," declares the LORD, "plans to prosper you and not to harm you, plans to give you hope and a future. Then you will call on me and come and pray to me, and I will listen to you. You will seek me and find me when you seek me with all your heart. (Jeremiah 29:11-13)

Jeremiah reminded all believers that God had a plan for him to be a prophet, but for Jeremiah to realize that plan, he had to seek Him with all of His heart and listen to Him. I will address both of these issues later in this book. The fact that in the first chapter of his book, Jeremiah writes, "The word of the LORD came to me, saying, "Before I formed you in the womb I knew you before you were born I set you apart; I appointed you as a prophet to the nations" (Jeremiah 1:4-8). Again, "the Bible illustrates God's call on Jeremiah before Jeremiah was born" (Sisson, 1986, p. 78). *We are reminded that we are created by God to do something for God.* As I will address later, Jeremiah 29:13 is critical to humans understanding their calling when Jeremiah writes, "you will seek me and find me when you seek me with all of your heart." No one will be able to discern God's will for their lives without understanding that they were created in God's image, redeemed by His one and only Son, and they have a relationship with Him from the moment of their salvation by the indwelling of His Holy Spirit (MacArthur, 2012). MacArthur suggests that no one can discern God's will for one's life without first knowing God personally. Second, one must make Jesus not only their Savior but also the Lord of their life. Third, one must seek Jesus with all their heart (MacArthur, 2012).

Stringfellow (2014) details over fifty Biblical characters who demonstrate God's specific vocational calling on their lives. For example, God called Noah to build the ark, Moses to lead the

> WE ARE REMINDED THAT WE ARE CREATED BY GOD TO DO SOMETHING FOR GOD.

Israelites out of captivity, Nehemiah to rebuild the wall in Jerusalem, Joshua to lead the Israelites into the Promised Land, the Disciples to follow Jesus, and Paul to be the Apostle to the Gentiles.

These characters from scripture represent normal ordinary people who *had a specific "call" on their lives by God and had to walk faithfully in obedience to fulfill God's will for their lives*. In fact, in the Bible, the Greek verb *kaleo,* which translated means "to call," appears 148 times in the New Testament. The three primary uses are:

1) Used by Jesus to "summon" or "invite" (to repentance, faith, salvation, or service)

2) Used by Paul to describe bringing a sinner to faith and salvation, and

3) a "call" to a specific function or office (vocation).

Many Bible characters who were called used their *spiritual gifts* to meet a specific *need* that God revealed to them and served a *need* that God *called* them specifically to fulfill. This is the Biblical model and formula demonstrated throughout scripture that I examined and now offer to help you discern God's vocational will for your life. I hope that when you discover your true Biblical calling, you will not become burned out, feel unfulfilled or unsettled about your current profession, suffer from anxiety, or feel like you are simply marking time with no specific purpose in life. God has entrusted goals, dreams, and aspirations to you. I deeply desire for you to discover them and walk obediently in them.

DECISION MAKING AND THE WILL OF GOD

Finally, before I conclude this section of the theological perspective of discovering God's individual vocational will for your life, no blog, journal article, or book would be complete without mentioning the most comprehensive dissertation, text, and twenty-fifth-anniversary edition of the book written on decision making and the will of God, *Decision Making and the Will of God,* by Garry Friesen.

Garry Friesen presented his opinions regarding decision-making and God's will in his dissertation to Dallas Theological Seminary in 1978.

Two years later, in 1980, Friesen published a book, *Decision Making and the Will of God*. This book created quite a debate among religious circles. In 2004, Frieson published a twenty-fifth anniversary updated edition of this work and addressed many of his critics within the updated text. This book had sold over 250,000 copies as of 2004.

Friesen (2004) writes that when it comes to God's will, there is a traditional view accepted by most Christian leaders, writers, and scholars, which states that God has three specific wills: a sovereign will, a moral will, and an individual will.

GOD'S SOVEREIGN WILL

Does God have a sovereign will? The traditional view says, "Yes," and Friesen (2004) agrees. God's sovereign will determine everything that happens in the universe (Daniel 4:35, Proverbs 16:33, 21:1, Revelation 4:11, Ephesians 1:11, Romans 9:19, 11:33-36, and Acts 2:23, 4:27-28). Philosophers and theologians for centuries have tried to figure out the mystery of God's sovereign will, but our finite human minds are simply incapable (Pink, 2001). Swindoll (1999) states that the key to understanding God's sovereignty is that you cannot. Swindoll (1999) and Friesen (2004) agree on this point. Swindoll (1999) further writes that God's sovereignty is a mystery held in the hands of a faithful God. Finally, Swindoll (1999) divides God's sovereignty into what God decrees and what God permits. Swindoll (1999) also clarifies that God allows evil things, but God is still sovereign over all. Swindoll (1999) also believes in the moral will and the individual will of God.

Jonathan Edwards, the greatest theologian and philosopher of British American Puritanism and the stimulator of the Great Awakening, writes in regards to God's sovereignty regarding the salvation of people, 'He not only is sovereign, and has a sovereign right to dispose and order in that affair; and He not only might proceed in a sovereign way, if He would, and nobody could charge Him with exceeding his right, but He actually does so; He exercises the right which He has." (Edwards, 2012).

There is one, however, who knows all of the answers. That One is "the blessed and only Sovereign, the King of kings, and Lord of lords (1 Timothy 6:15)." Scripture reveals five things about God's sovereign will.

God's sovereign will is:

1) Certain (will be fulfilled)
2) Detailed (includes all things)
3) Hidden (except when revealed by prophecy)
4) Supreme (without violating human responsibility or making God the author of sin)
5) Perfect (works all things together for God's glory and our good). (Friesen, 2004).

C.S. Lewis reminds people in his classic book, *Mere Christianity* (1996), that in God's sovereignty, He took the risk of creating beings who could choose sin. But fortunately for humanity, in God's sovereignty, He had already prepared the redemption that would be necessary.

The ultimate proof of God's sovereign will was presented at Calvary. Far from frustrating God's plan, the most wicked act ever committed – the willful murder of God's Son and Israel's Messiah – accomplished the central requirement of God's glorious plan of redemption (Friesen, 2004). The crucifixion was not God's plan B. A Savior was foreknown before the foundation of the world (1 Peter 1:20) and promised. At the same time, the forbidden fruit was still in Adam's mouth (Genesis 3:15).

The crucifixion was prophetically described in detail (Psalm 22), and the death of the Messiah was divinely interpreted as an offering for guilt some six hundred years before the event (Isaiah 53:3-12). Judas's betrayal was prophesied (Matthew 26:24, Acts 1:16) and foretold by Jesus at the Last Supper (Luke 22:21).

The time when the Messiah would be "cut off" was predicted by Daniel (Daniel 9:26). And in his Pentecost sermon, Peter declared that the very criminals who carried out the farcical trials accomplished God's predetermined plan (Acts 2:23). Herod, Pontius Pilate, the Gentiles, and Israel gathered against Jesus "to do whatever God's hand and purpose predestined to occur." (Acts 4:27-28). So, the final verdict is that no one can frustrate or change God's sovereign will and plan.

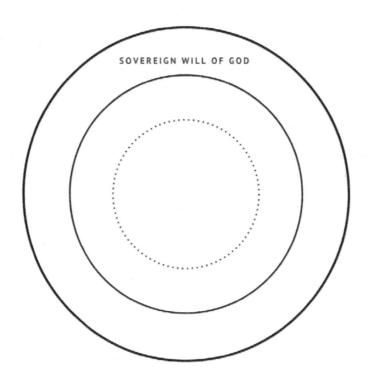

SOVEREIGN WILL OF GOD

GOD'S MORAL WILL

Does God have a moral will? The scriptures reveal the moral will of
God. Again, Friesen (2004) agrees. God's commands teach humanity
both what they should believe and how they should act (Romans 2:18,
1 Thessalonians 4:3, 5:18, and 2 Corinthians 6:14). Regarding one's
moral will, Dr. John Mitchell, one of the founders of Multnomah Bible
College in Portland, Oregon writes about one's moral will, "the only
will of God that must be discovered was never lost – it is just ignored
(Packer,1984)." J.I Packer's once described Christianity in North

America as being three thousand miles wide and a half an inch deep"
when it comes to the development of a moral will due to the lack of
Biblical emphasis by western Christianity (Gulley, 2002). Friesen
(2004) writes that while evangelicals agree about the reality of God's
moral will, they disagree on the extent to which that moral will
provides guidance in making specific decisions.

In his book *Discovering God's Will*, Ferguson (1992) writes that he does
not think God's will is hidden. So "discovering" is not what one might
expect in most books regarding God's
will. Most people who subscribe to the
traditional view of God's will may
believe that Ferguson (1992) never
answers how to discover God's will. He
does raise one's hope by using terms
like "perfect will" (p. 25) and "center of
God's will" (p. 85), but his meaning is different from what readers
might expect. Ferguson (1992) assumes that God desires one thing in
each decision, but he does not define it or show it in Scripture.
Ferguson argues that when Scripture correctly applies to the
individual situation, the result is living in God's will. He concludes
that the will of God is found by 1) direct commands of Scripture, 2)
principles found in Scripture, and 3) illustrations used in Scripture.
Therefore, "the chief need that believers have, is the increased

> THEREFORE, "THE CHIEF NEED THAT BELIEVERS HAVE, IS THE INCREASED FAMILIARITY WITH AND SENSITIVITY TO THE WISDOM FOUND IN GOD'S WORD."

familiarity with and sensitivity to the wisdom found in God's Word." (p. 31).

Friesen's (2004) opinion is that the traditional view holds that the Bible (God's moral will) gives most of the guidance needed to make a decision and that knowing God's individual will is essential for ultimately leading to the correct choice. Friesen (2004) argues that the Bible is sufficient to provide all guidance needed for a believer to know and do God's will and that there is no need to know God's essential will for the individual because an individual will does not exist. This opinion that God does not have an individual will is the epicenter of the debate between Friesen's (2004) view of God's will for decision-making and many others.

As it relates to theological anthropology, Friesen (2004) writes that the moral will of God is the expression, in behavioral terms, of the character of God. Ironically, he continues that God's moral will is precisely what Satan attacked in the Garden of Eden. Satan sought to usurp Eve by tempting her to be "like God." (Genesis 3:5). When, in fact, Adam and Eve were already "like God" and created in the image of God, which was God's design from the beginning (Bird, 1981). God desired humanity to reflect his likeness and glory on the finite level (Friesen, 2004). As Kilner (2018) writes, God's image was not altered at the fall of man, but man's ability to reflect God's glory was dimmed.

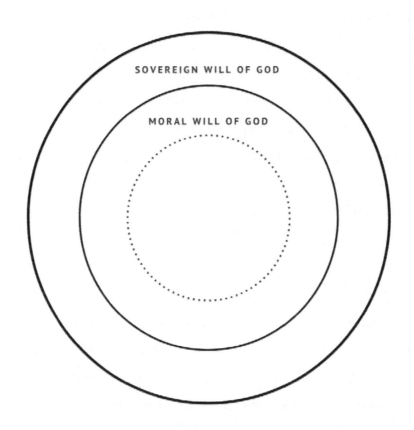

SOVEREIGN WILL OF GOD

MORAL WILL OF GOD

GOD'S INDIVIDUAL WILL

Does God have an individual will? Friesen (2004) argues for most of his 526 pages that "No," God does not have an individual will for believers. Friesen (2004) defines an individual will of the *traditional view* as "God's ideal, detailed life plan uniquely designed for each person." (Colossians 1:9, 4:14, Romans 12:2, Ephesians 5:17, 6:6, Proverbs 3:5-6, 16:6, Psalm 32:8, Genesis 24). God's guidance for decision-making is given through the indwelling of the Holy Spirit, who progressively reveals God's life plan to the heart of the believer through various means. This aspect of God's will is usually of most concern to those facing life's decisions.

One of the problems with this argument by Friesen is that he calls this the "traditional view" and claims that many Christians hold it, but many Christians today do not believe this concept. Most "traditional" Christians today would NOT say that God has an "ideal, detailed, life-pan uniquely designed for each person for *every single aspect of their lives*, and would agree with Friesen that many ordinary decisions that must be made in life are not "directly" outlined in scripture (where to live, who to marry, etc.). Friesen calls this *traditional view* the "dot" and claims that most Christians are striving "aimlessly" to find it because it does not exist (see the "traditional" view of God's individual will illustration below from Friesen's book).

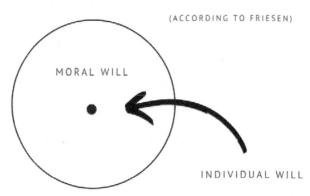

THE CENTER OF GOD'S WILL

(ACCORDING TO FRIESEN)

MORAL WILL

INDIVIDUAL WILL

I would agree with Friesen that God's Word and God's will is not that there is only ONE specific "right" choice for many of our day-to-day decisions that we must make in life (where to have lunch, what to wear, what time to get up, where to work out, etc.). However, when it comes to the bigger and more important decisions in life (like discerning God's vocational will for one's life), some information, inventories, assessments, and models can be implemented into Friesen's "way of wisdom" that are extremely helpful. My new model is one of them that can be added to this list.

As we will address later in this book, Friesen's "way of wisdom" is found in God's sovereign will and His moral will. Friesen claims that if Christians are operating in obedience inside these two wills, the way of wisdom states that you can operate *"freely"* inside this *"zone"* to make the best decision based on "evaluating data, devoting sufficient time to the process of decision making, seeking mature counsel, rightly applying scripture, and utilization of sound reasons (Friesen, p. 252).

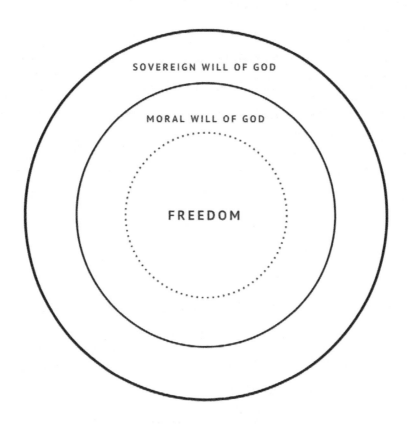

I agree with Friesen one hundred percent. My model requires these same "ways of wisdom" steps in each specific area of *passion, spiritual gifting, and needs assessment.* So, I would place my new model *"inside"*

his *"way of wisdom"* Freedom circle in his diagram, as we will discover towards the end of the book after you learn my model in the following chapters.

I would also add that when Friesen claims that God does not have an individual will for us, he is alone on an island, like Tom Hanks in Cast Away, merely communicating with Wilson, his fictitious volleyball companion. Many educators and scholars have written extensively about the existence of God having an individual will for believers. For example, in *How to Live the Full Adventure of Knowing and Doing the Will of God,* Blackaby and King (1994) elaborate on the seven principles outlined in Blackaby's previous best-selling work, *Experiencing God.* In this book, the authors highlight God's beautiful relationship with humans created in His image and how God's greatness is extolled as one's faith grows.

This book challenges readers to give complete dedication and absolute obedience to God as they submit to His will for their lives. They summarize that discovering God's will is a combination of discerning God's will from God through the Bible, prayer, and circumstances as the Holy Spirit leads, guides, and directs. Friesen (2004) disagrees with Blackaby and King (1994) strongly on this point, stating that people must be cautious of attempting to discern God's will from an "exegesis" of circumstances.

In MacArthur's (1994) book, *Reckless Faith*, MacArthur (1994) summarizes the objective guidelines of God's will. He writes, it is God's will that 1) we are saved (1 Timothy 2:3-4), 2) we are Spirit-filled (Ephesians 5:17-18), 3) we are sanctified (1 Thessalonians 4:3), 4) we are submissive (1 Peter 2:13-14), and 5) we suffer (1 Peter 4:19, Philippians 1:29, 2 Timothy 3:12), (p. 190). MacArthur (1994) summarizes that if these five things are the realities of your life, you do not need to worry about the decisions that you make in life. However, he does note that if all five of these things are true in a believer's life, a believer's decisions will not involve any directly forbidden choices in Scripture. He concludes that if all five elements are present, God's will should be running one's "wants" (p. 31).

Guinness (2003) writes that the phrase "the call" is what the conventional view uses to describe God's individual will for the life work of each person. However, for Guinness (2003), the call is the bedrock of the Christian life and commitment. It is almost what Friesen (2004) calls God's moral will. Guinness (2003) defines calling as" the truth that God calls us to Himself so decisively that everything we are, everything that we do, and everything that we have is invested with special devotion and dynamism lived out as a response to his summons and service." (p. 4).

Smith (1991) also argues for the existence of God's individual will. However, he defines God's individual will as seeking a rational biblically-based reason for the decisions that one makes.

Interestingly, Friesen (2004) states about Smith's (1991) book, if you would take out "individual will" in Smith's (1991) book and insert the phrase "Godly, wise decisions," then our two books would be almost identical. For example, Smith (1991) writes that one must first study Scripture to discern God's will. Then, one should use reason to make a logical choice about God's will, as opposed to looking for supernatural indications or purely intuitive impressions of his guidance." (p. 103).

Spurgeon (1862) writes that the great controversy that has divided the Christian church for ages has hinged upon the thorny question of "the will." Spurgeon writes, "I need not say of that conflict that it has made much mischief to the Christian church, undoubtedly it has, but I will rather say, that it has been fraught with incalculable usefulness, for it has thrust forward before the minds of Christians, precious truths, which, but for it, might have been kept in the shade. Spurgeon believes that the two great doctrines of human responsibility and divine sovereignty have both been brought out more prominently in the Christian church by the fact that there is a class of strong-minded hard-headed men who magnify sovereignty at the expense of responsibility and another earnest and useful class who uphold and maintain human responsibility often at the expense of divine sovereignty." This researcher finds it very interesting that this debate from 1862 still rages today.

Those looking for a simple formula for finding the "will of God" will not find it in Willard's (1999) book, *Hearing God: Developing a Conversational Relationship with God*, which covers a much broader scope of this subject, as indicated by the book's title, "developing a conversation with God." Willard (1999) believes that one needs to listen to God when He speaks to their inner being in His still, quiet voice. Willard (1999) offers dozens of pages on how to know when God is speaking through your own feelings, impressions, and thoughts. Friesen (2004) disagrees with this concept one hundred percent. Friesen even has an entire chapter in his book called impressions, where he strongly warns believers not to listen to their thoughts, feelings, and inner voice to determine God's will. Interestingly, Blackaby (1994) also agrees with Willard (1999), and both of these well-read, intelligent, and well-respected authors disagree with Friesen (2004).

Friesen (2004) is definitely in the minority of authors who deny the existence of an individual will for believers. The following sections will discuss how Friesen (2004) concludes that there is no individual will for believers and highlights the scripture he cites to make his argument while referencing potential flaws in his interpretation. This rebuttal of an individual will for people includes biblical characters who exhibit that God has an individual will and scriptures, which refute Friesen's (2004) conclusions.

FRIESEN'S ARGUMENT

An important point when discussing Friesen's (2004) denial of an individual will of God is his definition of individual will. As stated previously, Friesen's explanation of the traditional view of an individual will is "God's ideal, detailed life plan uniquely designed for each person." By this narrow definition, perhaps an individual will for a person could be debated. However, few writers in the literature on biblical guidance for decision-making equate this individual will with God's sovereign will. Obviously, God's sovereign will cannot be found in advance or missed. Friesen (2004), however, states, "My contention is that an individual will of God for every detail of a person's life is not found in scripture." (p. 41). So, why does Friesen (2004) write so strongly that an individual will does not exist? The following section will outline his arguments about how the evangelical community misunderstood the traditional view of an individual will.

Friesen (2004), however, says that events recorded in Scripture do not prove that God has an individual will for people. In fact, he summarizes his thoughts by stating the following four reasons based on Biblical examples: God does not have an individual will for people. First, Friesen (2004) cites that the number of recorded cases in Scripture is insufficient to constitute normative experience. I'm afraid I have to disagree with this conclusion. The biblical examples noted above, along with the stories of Abraham, Moses, Joseph, Esther, Nehemiah, Jeremiah, Isaiah, and many more, show clear scriptural evidence of God's individual will for people. So, Friesen (2004) says that God does not have an individual will for people when it has actually been recorded in a detailed fashion by multiple writers over hundreds of years in God's Word. Therefore, this conclusion is contrary to Scripture's truth.

Second, Friesen (2004) writes that biblical examples are not sufficiently comprehensive. He writes, "If God has an individual will for believers, then it should cover every decision made, and the biblical examples do not touch upon life's ordinary decisions." (p. 46). Friesen (2004) further writes, "Most of the instances in Acts had some direct bearing on the spread of the gospel, and God gave the specific leading to ensure evangelical outreach during the formative years of the church. In the book of Acts, there is no indication of any specific word from God on the ordinary decisions of life." (p. 47). However, just because the events of daily activities are not recorded in Scripture, like what these biblical characters had for lunch, what they were

47

wearing, and what time they got up in the morning, does not mean that those events did not occur.

Clearly, God orchestrated these events in their lives. Furthermore, their heartbeats, pulse, and respiratory rates are not recorded, so does this mean these men were not alive? It would have been impossible for the individual events for each one of these encounters to have been accurately recorded in Scripture. We are fortunate to have as many details and biblical examples as we have in the Bible. Many wish we had more information on God's direct interaction with humanity in the Old Testament and both Jesus (like his childhood) and the Holy Spirit's interaction with humanity (especially in the private life and study of Paul) in the New Testament.

Third, Friesen (2004) argues that God does not have an individual will for people because the biblical examples were recipients of specific guidance, and they occupied a special place in the outworking of God's program. Friesen (2004) further states that these biblical examples were people selected by God to play a significant role in His plan. One could argue that this is an individual's will. Furthermore, don't all people have the opportunity to play an essential role in the redemption of others and are invited, in fact, commanded to participate in the Great Commission? (Matthew 28:16-20).

Friesen (2004) references Peter and Paul as examples in Acts, apostles who received special revelation because of their unique office in the church. He also notes nonapostolic recipients of direct guidance – Phillip, Ananias, Cornelius, and the church at Antioch found themselves at a strategic historical crossroads in spreading the gospel beyond the house of Israel. Friesen (2004) concludes, "By virtue of their reception of divine revelation and their obedience to it, they became key figures in the worldwide propagation of the gospel. Examples of detailed divine guidance in Scripture are infrequent, limited in scope, and directed to persons who play a special role in God's program for the earth. Such selectivity on the part of God weakens rather than strengthens the support for the concept of an individual will for all people." (p.47).

Again, this conclusion by Friesen (2004) is questionable. There are numerous examples in Scripture (it is not infrequent) of detailed divine guidance (Mary, Joseph, Elizabeth, Martha, etc.). And what about the call of the twelve disciples? No one could argue that these men were not prominent leaders, kings, wealthy, influential, or in high positions (MacArthur, 2002). And Jesus, as a man walking along (and later on) the Sea of Galilee, called them to fulfill an individual and significant calling. It was not a bright light or a loud voice from heaven but a simple human (but divine) invitation. The truth is, one has no accurate way to measure the number of individual callings that people in the Bible received and obeyed because it was impossible to record back then, just as it is impossible to record here today the level of obedience of God's individual calling.

Finally, Friesen (2004) writes that the final flaw in biblical examples as a basis for an individual will is the means of communication. He claims that the traditional view holds that supernatural revelation is not the normative experience for all believers. Yet, he states that many Biblical examples supporting individual guidance involve supernatural revelation. In Acts, such guidance came through visions (9:10-16, 10:3-8, 10:17, 16:9-10, 18:9, 22:17-22), angelic messenger (8:26, 12:7-9, 27:23), physical miracle (8:39), an audible voice from God (8:29, 9:3-6, 10:19-20, 23:11), or a prophet who had received direct revelation (13:1-2, 21:10-11). Friesen (2004) is bold enough to write, "There are no recorded examples where detailed guidance was given through a means other than supernatural revelation." (p. 47). Again, this conclusion by Friesen (2004) is perplexing. Surly, Friesen (2004) is not insinuating that a supernatural revelation is necessary for a person to discern God's will.

God can call, guide, direct, and lead people in any way He desires. Mordechai sat out by the gate, and Esther begged him to fast and pray for three days and nights with her for God's sovereign will, moral will, and individual will to be done for whether or not to approach King

Xerxes without being summoned (Esther 4:15-16). There was no angel, bright light, or voice of God. Yet, God used Esther individually to save the Jews from Haman's plot. And this is just one biblical example, but many others are recorded in Scripture. And what about all of those that are not recorded? Friesen (2004) makes another bold and declarative statement, "There are no examples in scripture of ordinary believers making decisions in a manner outlined by the traditional view." (p. 48). Respectfully, I have already provided one.

Finally, I find it very interesting that in the revised edition of Friesen's (2004) book, he answers several questions from critics. One of these questions is, "Wouldn't you agree that God's sovereign will applies to individuals as well as every individual thing that happens? How can you say that there is no individual will of God? Friesen (2004) answers by saying, yes, there is an individual will encompassed by the sovereign will. *But since that is not what the traditional view means by that terminology, I have refrained from saying so until now to avoid confusion.* So, in conclusion, even Friesen believes that there IS an individual will of God, just framed within God's sovereign will, which, of course, is never changing.

CONCLUSION

This chapter has identified several critical works in literature to support the Biblical theory that all people are created *by* God, *for* God, and to have a relationship *with* God. Therefore, I would suggest that you cannot discern God's vocational will for your life without knowing God and making Jesus your Lord and Savior. Many people will never experience God's will for their lives because they will never surrender to Him, place their trust and faith in Him, and allow the Holy Spirit's presence to lead them. The indwelling and the leadership of the Holy Spirit in your life is the only way that peace can be realized here on earth and in the presence of God in eternity in Heaven.

However, many people who know Jesus Christ and have accepted Him as their Lord and Savior still have trouble discovering God's vocational will for their lives. You may be one of them. So, merely knowing Jesus and following Jesus does not necessarily mean that you know how to systematically identify God's individual vocational calling for your life. Many people still move aimlessly from location to location, job to job, and friend group to friend group. Thompson and Miller-Perrin (2003) write that vocation is a concept familiar to society's sacred and secular constituents. Those holding the secular perspective define vocation as one's work, career, or occupation.

In contrast, many Christians view vocation as a *calling* from God. God calls a person "with a holy calling, not according to our works, but according to his purpose and grace" (2 Timothy 1:9). This holy calling refers to hearing and understanding God's voice in your life and obeying the summons given. Thus, your vocation or calling brings divine meaning and purpose to the life of a Christian (Thompson & Miller-Perrin, 2003).

When this occurs, I suggest that not only are you more fulfilled and experiencing the inner peace that comes from a life of obedience, but the Kingdom of God will be expanding here on earth (Matthew 28:19) until the Lord returns (Acts 1:11). This three-step model, which will help people discover that they are created by God, to glorify God, and to understand God's individual vocational will for their lives, involves you discovering your passion, discerning your spiritual gifts, and evaluating where there is a need in this world for someone with your passion and spiritual gift.

It should be noted that it is also the will of God for all believers to be active in sharing the gospel of Jesus Christ with others (Matthew 28:16-20), regardless of their God-ordained individual vocation. If you currently are not a believer in Jesus Christ, I encourage you to visit TrueLife.org, which contains video answers to some of life's hardest questions and several clear-cut video presentations of the birth, life, death, burial, and resurrection of Jesus Christ, explaining who Jesus was, why He came to earth, and what he accomplished for all people while He was here.

If you are a believer, I would remind you that in a recent survey conducted by Lifeway (2022), 73% of non-believers stated that they would be willing to have a conversation with a stranger about spiritual matters. In that same study, it was discovered that less than one percent of believers are willing to talk to a stranger about their faith. This is a problem.

So, if you are a believer, I encourage you to prayerfully ask the Lord to help you be more observant, compassionate, and willing to share the truth of the gospel with others. TrueLife.org is also a great website to train and equip you for this mission. It offers incredible resources like "Evangelism Boot Camp" to help you prepare for these opportunities to share the truth of the gospel with others that you encounter every day. Jesus, of course, is the best model of sharing the gospel with others as he traveled and met others throughout his earthly ministry.

CHAPTER THREE

The Theoretical and Sociological
Perspective of Calling

THEORETICAL PERSPECTIVE

But discovering God's individual vocational will is more than merely a theological discussion. Theoretically, many scholars have also examined and wrestled with the issue of vocational calling. The conceptual definition of calling represents perhaps the most controversial issue within the theoretical literature. Although a calling has been described as an orientation (Bellah et al., 1986), mindset, or perspective (Dik & Duffy, 2009), many say that a calling is a psychological construct that may be folded into more extensive career theories or interventions, rather than a new theory of career development or career counseling - analogous to well-studied vocational constructs like self-efficacy or outcome expectations. In their review of definitions across the humanities and social sciences, Dik and Duffy (2009) identified three components that, when combined, were emblematic of a calling in the work domain.

The first was the notion of an *external summons* - that if an individual feels called to a specific type of work, this necessarily implies a caller, which may come in the form of a higher power, the needs of society, a family legacy, the needs of one's country, or any other force external to the individual. This component is consistent with the literal meaning of "calling" and how it has historically been used in the context of work.

The second component is that one's approach to work aligns with one's broader sense of *purpose in life*; for such individuals, work is either a source of purpose or a life domain that allows for a sense of purpose.

The third component is that a person's career is *prosocial-oriented*; individuals with a calling use their profession to directly or indirectly *help others or advance the greater good.*

The combination of these three elements – an external summons, meaning/purpose, and prosocial motivation – is what distinguishes *calling* from closely related constructs such as work centrality (Dubin, 1956), work commitment (Loscocco, 1989), work engagement (Kahn, 1990), meaningful work (Rosso et al., 2010), and prosocial work behaviors (Grant, 2007, Grant, 2008).

It is important to note that "secular" sociologists and not theologians point out these three constructs. Therefore, even non-theological researchers recognize the importance of these three constructs that form the basis for my three-step model. So, my model combines three critical elements, theologically and sociologically.

Furthermore, Dik and Duffy (2009) recommended that individuals examine a calling along a spectrum (not merely having one or not having one), introduced a distinction between seeking and experiencing a calling, described calling as an ongoing process rather than something to be discovered once and for all, and proposed that callings often change over time. This conceptualization of calling has informed the two most widely used instruments to assess calling in empirical research (Dik et al., 2012).

In these studies, the participants described a remarkable range of origins of the calling, some external (e.g., God, a higher power), some internal (e.g., one's own interests, skills, values, and passions), and some that may fall in the overlap of internal and external, such as a sense of destiny (e.g., what one is meant to do). Some scholars have argued that these internal source conceptualizations are a better fit for how the construct is viewed in the current culture, noting that many individuals who feel a calling do not identify an external caller but rather point to working in a career that aligns with their strongest internal *passions* (Dobrow & Tosti-Kharas, 2011; Elangovan et al., 2010; Hagmaier & Abele, 2012; Hall & Chandler, 2005). Accordingly, several calling instruments have been developed, conceptualizing *calling as arising from an inner voice or sense of passion* (Dobrow & Tosti-Kharas, 2011; Hagmaier & Abele, 2012).

Since 2007 approximately 40 studies have been completed examining how calling links to work-related and general well-being outcomes. Dik and Duffy (2009) reviewed results from these studies across six primary domains: the prevalence of calling, career maturity, work outcomes, domain satisfaction, well-being, and the distinction between perceiving vs. living a calling. Each study's particular instruments were discussed, given how calling has been conceptualized and measured. Apart from early categorization studies, most studies have been based on Dik and Duffy's (2009) conceptualization of *calling*.

To date, however, there is *no universal agreement* over the definition, origins, or developmental trajectory of career calling (Elangovan et al., 2010; Hall & Chandler, 2005; Wrzesniewski, 2012). Generally, it is agreed that adults with a *calling* approach their work with a *stronger sense of meaning, purpose, and fulfillment* and have a greater desire *to contribute to others* and the community through their occupational activities (Dik & Duffy, 2009; Hall & Chandler, 2005; Steger et al.,

2010). This understanding has guided the development of several career calling measures, although not all of these measures have strong theoretical underpinnings, are not assessing developmental progress towards a future career, focus mainly on those in the workforce, or need further investigation to confirm their psychometric properties (Duffy et al., 2012; Duffy & Sedlacek, 2007; Rosso et al., 2010). Notably, no scales, methods, or models were developed specifically to assess the career calling in emerging adults, whose main developmental focus is discovering their future careers. So, my model and dissertation study was conducted to develop and validate this new practical three-step model to meet this purpose. And as you will see, it was remarkably successful in assisting these emerging adults.

SOCIOLOGICAL PERSPECTIVE

Secular callings originate within the individual (Hall & Chandler, 2005; Rosso et al., 2010; Wrzesniewski et al., 2009) and are central to one's identity and unique talents (Dobrow, 2007; Hall & Chandler, 2005; Novak, 1996). These perspectives recognize people's efforts to find a sense of personal, self-relevant meaning (Bellah et al., 1985; Dobrow, 2004), which can apply to people of any faith or none (Dobrow, 2007), and can reflect a desire to contribute to the community or larger society in some way (Dobrow, 2004; Elangovan et al., 2010; Steger et al., 2010). Individuals can understand their callings as a consuming passion towards a specific domain, which can generate a strong sense of urgency, longevity, and domain-specific competence (Dobrow, 2004, 2007; Dobrow & Tosti-Kharas, 2011), personal mission or a quest for self-fulfillment and enjoyment (Dobrow, 2004; Hall & Chandler, 2005; Novak, 1996), or a work orientation, where work is considered inseparable from one's life (Bellah et al., 1986; Wrzesniewski et al., 1997).

Rather than seeing calling as something stable in the individual (Dobrow, 2004), Hall and Chandler (2005) argued that, next to a strong sense of purpose, individuals with a calling needed to be *internally driven* by their own values and identity, motivated to follow a path (i.e., be self-directed), and be self-exploring, adaptive, and confident in maneuvering in the career path. This view highlights the ongoing processes of goal-setting, goal-pursuit, adaptation, and development of a calling. In other words, developing and achieving a calling involves personal agency or orientation that is goal- and action-orientated and includes self-motivational and adaptive processes necessary to reach one's goals (Bandura, 1991; Elangovan et al., 2010). In the careers area, adaptive processes include career exploration, introspection, reflection, and relational activities, such as discussions with parents and friends (Hall & Chandler, 2005). As noted earlier, parents, mentors, and friends currently have no proven model to direct people to in this pursuit.

Career calling has also been distinguished from passion (Vallerand et al., 2003), flow (Csikszentmihalyi, 1990), and work engagement (Kahn, 1990). These constructs exist on an episodic basis rather than more enduring, stable, and long-term, which characterizes a calling (Dik & Duffy, 2009; Dobrow & Tosti-Kharas, 2011; Elangovan et al., 2010; Hall & Chandler, 2005).

Career calling has also been differentiated from other work constructs, such as work commitment (Loscocco, 1989), career salience (Greenhaus, 1971), and career hope (Diemer & Blustein, 2007), which do not capture the core meaningfulness, purpose, and prosocial components of calling. Last, some concepts focus on a narrow aspect of calling but do not capture its whole, complex nature. For example, career identity, orientation, and work preference are considered important career constructs, but they do not encompass all components of a calling (Amabile et al., 1994; Dobrow, 2004; Hall & Chandler, 2005).

CAREER CALLING AND EMERGING ADULTS

Emerging adulthood is the transition period from adolescence to early adulthood (i.e., approximately 18 to 25 years; Arnett, 2000). During this period, existing goals end, and new, more salient goals regarding study, career, and family life relevant to adulthood are developed and become the main focus (Havighurst, 1953/1961). Appraising goals in these areas as essential and controllable, and establishing plans and actions to achieve them, can be used as markers of positive development and adaptation for this age group and translate into positive outcomes for current well-being and future functioning (Shulman & Nurmi, 2010).

Developing a career calling reflects conscious and unconscious processes around goal setting and goal pursuit (Bandura, 1991; Locke & Latham, 1990); that is, career calling becomes salient for emerging adults as they formulate their career goals and engage in preparatory career actions that are focused on achieving meaningful work as an adult (Berg et al., 2010; Duffy & Sedlacek, 2010; Hall & Chandler, 2005; Nurmi, 1993). From this perspective, a career calling reflects higher-order goals, is more abstract, and has a longer-term view, in contrast to lower-level, more concrete, and short-term goals, which are how higher-order goals are achieved (Lord et al., 2010).

Consistent with this view, career calling is increasingly regarded as a developmental and dynamic construct (Elangovan et al., 2010; Weiss et al., 2004), which begins before one enters the workplace and strengthens as one matures (Wrzesniewski, 2012). Thus, the manifestation of career calling in emerging adults who have not yet formally entered the workforce and are still developing and deciding on a future direction will differ from adults who have selected their careers and entered the workforce.

Based on this developmental and goal-setting perspective (Bandura, 1991; Havighurst, 1953/1961; Locke & Latham, 1990), career calling in emerging adulthood can be represented as a mostly self-set, salient, higher-order career goal, which generates meaning and purpose for the individual, and which has the potential to be strengthened (or weakened) by engaging in goal-directed, career-preparatory actions and adaptive processes aimed at meeting this goal. This definition is consistent with other conceptualizations that view calling as a context-specific goal (Duffy & Dik, 2013) and promotes personal agency as the means for successfully pursuing it (Elangovan et al., 2010; Hall & Chandler, 2005; Dobrow, 2004).

Additionally, research on calling has been increasingly conducted on living a calling and the experiences of individuals once they've discovered their callings (Duffy, Bott, Allan, Torrey, & Dik, 2012b; Duffy & Autin, 2013; Duffy, Allan, Autin, & Bott, 2013), yet very little is known about how callings develop in the first place, among Millennials or anyone else (Duffy & Dik, 2013). After conducting a literature review on callings, Duffy and Dik (2013) concluded that the work in calling research is a growing area. Yet, gaps remain that need to be further addressed for a more complete understanding of this construct. Duffy and Dik (2013) conclude the "…role of the perceived source in how a sense of calling develops is not yet well understood..." (p. 429).

In the same fashion, Horton (2009) reports that discerning God's individual will for one's life covers a multitude of areas, in addition to merely what one wants to be when one grows up. Horton (2009) writes one of the most significant challenges facing high school students is making difficult decisions that will significantly impact their future. These decisions include what extra-curricular activities to become involved in, friendship choices, dating practices, which college or vocational school to attend, what program of study to pursue, which career path to follow, and more. The decision-making process becomes even more critical over the next several years as they face choices about marriage, graduate programs, specific job opportunities, or relocation to a new area. "To make matters more complicated, the number of possibilities in each area has multiplied in recent years" (Horton, 2009, p. 7).

Schwartz (2005) argues that those in affluent countries suffer from "choice overload," which results in a decreased sense of well-being. Schwartz (2005) documents how such a bewildering number of choices can lead to depression and even suicide in its more extreme form. "Choice overload causes confusion, anxiety, and decision-making paralysis" (Schwartz, 2005, pp. 201ff.).

Finally, Schwartz (2005) writes that the discernment process becomes even more complicated for Christian youth who desire to make choices according to God's will. Not only are they confronted with a multitude of options, but these students also have the added burden of determining whether or not their choices align with God's plan or purpose for their lives. Research offers no proven method or strategy to help these students choose God's will for their lives.

Horton (2009) writes that most Christian students are open to God's direction in their lives but are often confused about *how to discern* what precisely God would have them do. "Thus, a significant responsibility for working with these students is to equip them to think through critical principles for spiritual discernment and decision making" (Horton, 2009, p. 7). However, each mentor in this role is left to their own opinion, life experience, or limited career counseling expertise to help these students because *no model or method* for assisting them exists.

Galotti and Mark (1994) note that a significant determining factor in helping students decide what they want to become when they grow up is determined by the college or university they attend (influenced heavily by a faculty member, their peers, and their peer social circles). Galotti and Mark (1994) further note that the college or university a student decides to attend is usually determined during one's junior or senior year in high school.

In the United States, over two million students, their families, and relevant school personnel confront this time-consuming and expensive decision each year, spending over 50 hours investigating information (exclusive of campus visits) and approximately $1,500 indirect costs of preparing materials and gathering information (Litten, 1982). The collegiate choice has long-term ramifications for family ties, friendships, spouse decisions, need for loans, the probability of admission to graduate or professional school, social status, and vocational career paths (Boyer, 1987; Fischer et al., 1987; Litten, 1991). No method or model for discerning God's will is available to help families make this important choice. And college choice can be a critical component for one's long-term development and preparation to live a life vocationally in the center of God's will.

Many life-long decisions, such as vocation, marriage, and long-term friendships, are formed during the higher education classroom experience. In addition, many professional connections and personal experiences during these collegiate years contribute significantly to one's future vocational choice, place of employment, and even geographical location.

But, after this exhausting process of choosing a college, research also indicates that since high school seniors and first-year college students do not have an effective method for discerning God's vocational will, an estimated 20 to 50 percent of students enter college as undecided majors (Gordon, 1995) and according to the National Center for Educational Statistics, an estimated 80 percent of students change their major at least once, and the average college student *changes their major three times* before graduation (Astin & Panos, 1969; Theophilides et al., 1984; Kramer et al., 1994). Students who change their college majors are referred to as "major changers" in the education literature. Peterson (2006) states that a satisfactory model for explaining student behavior related to choosing majors has eluded educational analysts. The reasons students change their major and make new decisions are also insufficiently documented in the literature. Therefore, my model could save students valuable time and parents substantial financial resources.

BASED ON EXTENSIVE RESEARCH, I WOULD SUGGEST THAT MANY CHRISTIAN COLLEGE STUDENTS CHANGE THEIR MAJORS BECAUSE THEY HAVE NOT FIGURED OUT GOD'S VOCATIONAL WILL FOR THEIR LIVES.

Many educators are also unclear about how students make their initial major choices (Bertram, 1996; Hu, 1996). There is even more uncertainty about why students change their majors (Kramer et al., 1994). Based on extensive research, I would suggest that many

Christian college students change their majors because they have not figured out God's vocational will for their lives. And they have not figured out God's vocational will for their lives because they have not been given a method, model, or strategy to assist them in discovering this vital calling.

St. John (2000) perhaps summarizes the process of choosing a major best, "there is, perhaps, no college decision that is more thought-provoking, gut-wrenching, and rest-of-your life oriented-or disoriented-than the choice of a major" (St. John, 2000, p. 22). Roese and Summerville (2005) cite meta-analytical evidence that Americans' most frequently identified life regret is choosing their college major. Perhaps this regret is because many working adults are currently performing jobs they do not enjoy and merely paying their bills because they had no exposure to a practical and systematic plan for discovering God's individual vocational plan for their lives.

Hill and Miller (1981) write that many middle-aged Americans, ages 35 to 50, are currently working in a job that they are unsatisfied with, feel trapped, have no passion for, or just marking time. Schein (1978) states, "what is, from the point of view of the organization, simply "turnover" may be, from the point of view of the individual, a major transition crisis involving a search for one's occupational niche" (Schein, 1978, p. 172).

What do these researchers and studies all have in common? Their research concludes that most high school students, college students, and even many middle-aged adults have no proven method or reliable model for discerning God's will for their lives, much less for determining God's individual vocational will. While many parents, teachers, school guidance counselors, and even ministers attempt to answer this question for others, research indicates that most people answer this question based on their own lives or by pointing out successful leaders in various professions, but the vocational destination of others does not explain their journey or path to get there.

As stated, historically, no proven model or research study identifies how emerging adults can discern God's ordained individual vocational will for their lives. Theologically, God does have this will, and it can be discovered. Theoretically, one must consider many constructs (theologically and theoretically) in this process. And sociologically, a practical and proven model is needed.

CONCLUSION

As stated in this section, no proven model or research study historically identifies how emerging adults can discern God's ordained individual vocational will for their lives. Theologically, God does have this will, and it can be discovered. Theoretically, one must consider many constructs (theologically and theoretically) in this process. And sociologically, a practical and proven model is needed. Therefore, I conducted this validation study to collect and analyze data to determine if my three-step practical model was effective in helping these college students 18-25 years old (emerging adults in the literature) discover their individual vocational calling. I deeply desire for people to know God intimately and serve Him faithfully here on earth until they meet their Savior face-to-face and provide people a model to discover their vocational calling and leaders a model to assist others in this quest. Therefore, this book is significant for several reasons.

First, most Christian parents and leaders do not have a valid and reliable Biblically-based model to assist teenagers and college students in answering an extraordinarily vital and common question, "What is God's vocational will for my life?" (Ng et al., 2010).

Second, while the literature is extensive regarding the theology of God's vocational will, there is little literature, and currently, no existing model to help teenagers and college students discover God's vocational will for their lives (Duffy & Dik, 2009).

Third, my study can become the baseline model for many future studies in helping teenagers and college students live fulfilled lives of obedience because they have a practical three-step model they can complete independently (Duffy & Dik, 2009; Dobrow & Tosti-Kharas, 2011). Of course, discussing these steps with trusted and influential mentors from one's Christian community is another vital element of accurately discerning these three critical ingredients. This model would depend on a person having a congruent picture of who they are as a person in Christ and their ability and willingness to answer the assessment questions for each element genuinely and honestly (Ryan & Deci, 2001; Shaw & Gupta, 2004).

Therefore, this book is significant because it helps both individuals seeking God's vocational will and provides an instrument for Christian leaders who are often faced with assisting others in answering this vital question (Hall & Chandler, 2005).

SECTION TWO

PASSION

I hope that after you learn this new three-step practical model, you can use it to discover your God-ordained individual vocational calling. Then, I hope that you can practice this calling utilizing your passion and spiritual gifts to meet a need in our world. When this occurs, you may experience a life of physical, mental, emotional, and spiritual peace here on earth, and receive the crown promised in Heaven to those who live a life of faithful obedience (James 1:12, 1 Peter 5:4). The first step in this three-step process is for you to discover your God-ordained passion.

The following chapters will provide a brief historical, philosophical, scientific, and sociological perspective of passion. In addition, these chapters will also offer a few leadership principles, quotes, examples of passionate leaders, and three methods for discovering your God-given passion.

CHAPTER FOUR

Passion: A Historical and Philosophical Perspective

James (1997) states that scholars did not take time to ponder the origin of passion in ancient Greece, as it was accepted that it came from the gods. For example, in Homer's *Iliad*, a god restrains Achilles' anger when Agamemnon takes his mistress. For Plato (427-348 BC), passion was considered bad for people because it entailed a passivity devoid of reason and typically outside one's control. Plato opposed passion to reason and believed that one must become aware of one's passions because passion always overruled reason. Aristotle (384-322 BC) agreed with Plato that one's passions entailed a loss of reason. However, Aristotle suggested that passions were not necessarily terrible as they represented one of our most human characteristics derived from our experience. Aristotle also concluded that people should not be ashamed of their passions but must control them (James, 1997).

Next followed a period in which three new schools of thought took up the philosophical study of passion. Stoics held the first position. They agreed with Plato that passions were terrible and should be controlled by one's will. According to Hunt (1993):

> The next school of thought was introduced and held by Epicureans. They believed that not all passions were bad and that some were good. This position originated in the work of Epicurus (341-270 BC), who believed that pleasure is the beginning and the ending of life (p. 70).

Interestingly, the Epicureans were also the ones who first conceived two types of passion – pleasure and pain. This distinction between these two types of passion would then be used throughout history. As this author will note later, this is one of the premises of Vallerand's (2015) Dualistic Passion Model. Finally, the Romans held the third Stoic perspective, which ruled the world after the Greeks. The Stoic view was in line with their rugged way of life. Philosophers such as Seneca (3BC– 65AD) and Epictetus (60–120 AD) recommended the rejection of passion and pursuing abnegation, and passively accepting one's situation. Galen (130-201 AD), the Greek personal physician of Roman Emperor Marcus Aurelius, was a significant contributor to this work. He wrote *The Diagnosis and the Cure of the Soul's Passions.* In short, he agreed with both Plato's and Aristotle's ideas and recommended the control of passions through reason (James, 1997).

THE SCIENCE OF PASSION

Vallerand (2015) writes that the concept of passion is one people regularly use to describe their interests, and yet there is no broad theory that can explain the development and consequences of passion for activities across people's lives. Vallerand (2015) writes that philosophers, playwrights, film directors, and writers have examined the role of passion in people's lives for centuries. He notes, "From Shakespeare's *Romeo and Juliette* to Mel Gibson's *Passion of the Christ*, passion has been repeatedly celebrated in plays, movies, and popular writings throughout the centuries" (p.4).

Vallerand (2015) adds that there are several types of passion. For example, passion may mean a willingness to endure suffering. It is essential to understand the etymology of the word passion. "In both Greek, *pathos*, and Latin, *patio*, passion refers to suffering" (p. 5). Therefore, what is implied is that being passionate may lead one to suffer. As an example, Christians often refer to the passion of Christ and the fact that he had to endure his sufferings while pursuing his quest for the ultimate salvation of humanity through his crucifixion. Vallerand (2015) writes that "this type of passionate suffering has remained as an example of how to passively suffer and to accept one's fate" (p. 5) stoically. This concept is highlighted in Duckworth, Peterson, Matthews, and Kelly's (2007) study. They conclude that "one's persistence toward a goal in the face of adversity, displaying grit, is often equated with passion" (p. 274).

Braumeister et al. (1993) describe another form of suffering often associated with passion as a situation in which one is prevented from being united with the object of one's passion. For example, despair, anxiety, or even depression experienced by the passionate lover being rejected by the object of their love has been reported to be quite intense. This area of passion is represented in suffering by describing the person desperately trying not to succumb to their inner inkling to engage in illicit passionate activity. For instance, many passionate individuals can vividly describe the emotional pain and suffering they have experienced while trying to avoid partaking in a potentially harmful activity like drinking alcohol or gambling.

Closely related to a passion for suffering, people often experience intensely emotional situations. Passionate people may riot, protest, destroy property, or even harm others in a heightened emotional state (Horowitz, 2001). Well-publicized examples of this passion are usually negatively driven by the media or social media outlets. These types of episodes are often fueled by hatred or anger.

CONCLUSION

This chapter provided you with a historical and philosophical perspective of passion. Historically, passion has been investigated, written about, and driven actions since 427 BC. For Plato (427-348 BC), passion was considered bad for people because it entailed a passivity devoid of reason and typically outside one's control. However, Aristotle suggested that passions were not necessarily terrible as they represented one of our most human characteristics derived from our experience. Aristotle also concluded that people should not be ashamed of their passions but must control them (James, 1997).

When it comes to the science of passion, Vallerand (2015) writes that the concept of passion is one people regularly use to describe their interests, and yet there is no broad theory that can explain the development and consequences of passion for activities across people's lives. Vallerand (2015) writes that philosophers, playwrights, film directors, and writers have examined the role of passion in people's lives for centuries. He notes, "From Shakespeare's *Romeo and Juliette* to Mel Gibson's *Passion of the Christ*, passion has been repeatedly celebrated in plays, movies, and popular writings throughout the centuries" (p.4).

CHAPTER FIVE

What Passion Tells Us About People

In the first empirical study on passion for activities, Vallerand and Houlfort (2003) found that most participants (around 84%) were passionate about a given activity. They note, "Therefore, having passion for an activity is not limited to the happy few; rather, it characterizes most people. Furthermore, people can be passionate about several different activities" (p. 9). Vallerand and Houlfort (2003) also polled over 500 college-aged students, who all indicated being moderately passionate about at least one of the 150 activities provided on a list. These activities ranged from various sports, types of exercising, playing a musical instrument, reading, and even spending time with friends. The conclusion of this study revealed that students who are passionate about an activity voluntarily spent an average of *eight hours* a week participating in this activity. In addition, this study told the authors what type of activities these students were passionate about and how these students think, feel, and prioritize their lives and their schedules around these activities. "This study was not about the activities themselves but about how passion drives prioritizing time to perform them. Because the study of passion entails going into people's lives, researchers learn about the content and the process of people's decision-making processes for their lives as well" (p. 9).

HOW PASSION DRIVES SUCCESS

Beyond discovering people's lives and how they make decisions, the scientific study of passion can also tell us what successful people have in common. Specifically, research should tell us if those who thrive and excel do so because of their passion. Although philosophers, writers, and others may suggest that passion is crucial for various outcomes, such as performance and happiness, only scientific psychological research can determine if this is the case. Passion research can allow us to go beyond common sense and identify the role of *passion in people's optimal functioning.*

Seligman and Csikszentmihalyi (2000), who founded the field of positive psychology, asked a straightforward question, "How can people's lives be most worth living" (p. 27)? In short, the issues these authors addressed were what makes people happy? According to Seligman and Csikszentmihalyi, positive psychology aims to scientifically study and identify the factors that facilitate happiness. However, Ryan & Deci (2001) point out that the definition of happiness is a complex issue that has been debated for millennia. Dr. Vallerand (2015) summarizes that two broad perspectives of happiness have emerged. The first view, hedonic, holds that one needs to feel good (hedonism) to be happy. The other, eudemonic, believes that one needs to grow psychologically and reach one's full potential (eudemonism), which means to be optimally functioning.

So, what factors lead to reaching your full potential and being happy? Peterson (2006) lists several factors contributing to optimal performance and happiness. Vallerand, Gousse-Lessard, & Verner-Filion (2011) and Vallerand & Verner-Filion (2013) take the position that being passionate about a meaningful activity (or object or even a person) can provide joy and meaning to one's life that contributes to having a life worth living. For example, having a passion for playing a musical instrument or promoting a cause dear to your heart can lead you to self-realization and fulfillment. Thus, engaging in an activity that we are passionate about can make us feel good (hedonism), can help us achieve self-growth (eudemonic) as we progress in that activity, and may also contribute to other dimensions of our life, such as experiencing positive emotions, experiencing positive relationships, and achieving high-performance outcomes. In conclusion, Vallerand (2015) states that:

> Not only is passion important because it provides meaning and purpose to our lives, but it is also important because it is one

of the ways people can access the psychological processes known in positive psychology to facilitate well-being. (p.10)

PASSION CAN ALSO LEAD TO NEGATIVE BEHAVIOR

As positive as passion can be in helping one achieve optimal performance and happiness, passion can also lead to negative behavior patterns. Vallerand (2015) points out that most people know someone passionate and unhappy. These people seem to suffer and even make those around them suffer. Vallerand writes, "As positive and productive as passion can be, passion can also arouse negative emotions, lead to inflexibility, rigidity, and interfere with a balanced and successful life" (p. 11). Vallerand, who agrees with many philosophers, believes there seems to be a duality of passion that can bring out the best and the worst in people. This recognition is critical because Vallerand's high performance that the positive and the negative effects of passion are two sides of the same coin – the passion coin –must be considered to understand how passion may contribute to or detract from optimal functioning. After extensive research in various personal and professional fields, Vallerand's (2015) recognition of the two sides of passion led to the development of his Dualistic Model of Passion.

CONCLUSION

In this chapter, we investigated what passion tells us about people. We first learned that passion drives behavior. In the study polling over 500 college students, passion led to choosing activities for over eight hours a week of their limited discretionary time.

Next, we discovered how passion also drives success and happiness. Dr. Vallerand (2015) summarizes that two broad perspectives of happiness have emerged. The first view, hedonic, holds that one needs to feel good (hedonism) to be happy. The other, eudemonic, believes one needs to grow psychologically and reach one's full potential (eudemonism), which means optimal functioning.

Finally, we learned that passion could also lead to negative behavior. Vallerand writes, "As positive and productive as passion can be, passion can also arouse negative emotions, lead to inflexibility, rigidity, and interfere with a balanced and successful life" (p. 11).

CHAPTER SIX

The Dualistic Model of Passion

Vallerand (2015) presents a complete presentation of the Dualistic Model of Passion (DMP) and the empirical evidence that supports it. He proposes two types of passion: harmonious passion, which remains under the person's control, and obsessive passion, which controls the person. While harmonious passion typically leads to adaptive behaviors, the obsessive form of passion leads to less adaptive and, at times, maladaptive behaviors.

For example, Srikant & Sadachar (2018) note that harmonious passion refers to feeling the choice of engaging in the activity that one loves and is hypothesized to lead to more adaptive outcomes. On the other hand, obsessive passion reflects internal pressure to participate in an activity one loves. These two types of passion answer the paradox raised by philosophers on the seemingly contradictory positive and negative outcomes engendered by passion. Vallerand (2015) highlights the effects of these two types of passion on several psychological phenomena, such as cognition, emotions, performance, relationships, aggression, and violence.

Vallerand (2015) concludes that passion is different from emotion. Passion can be both positive and negative. The role that passion plays in the psychology of a person is powerful. Harmonious passion for a given activity can produce sustainable positive effects on one psychological well-being. Such results are not seen with obsessive passion. Passion is required for high-level performance; both types can contribute to this through different psychological processes. Although both forms of passion can facilitate creativity, harmonious passion seems to do much more than obsessive passion. Regarding societal outcomes like politics, religion, and the environment, harmonious passion typically leads to the most adaptive effects. In contrast, obsessive passion usually leads to less favorable and sometimes even maladaptive societal outcomes.

PASSION CAN BE BOTH POSITIVE AND NEGATIVE

A CHRISTIAN PERSPECTIVE ON PASSION

Hybels (2007) contends that "holy discontent occurs when one is so stirred by something (a cause, an injustice, etc.) that one simply has to do something" (p.13). He explains that one cannot go another minute, much less another day, without taking action when one is passionate about something. Hybels (2007) calls this passion. He writes that people are passionate about sports teams, jobs, social injustice, politics, clean drinking water, education, a cure for cancer, electric cars, traveling, teenagers, babies, elderly, unwed mothers inner-city areas, social media, and even religion.

In a follow-up book written five years later, Hybels (2012) writes, "Without a hint of exaggeration, the ability to discern divine direction has saved me from a life of sure boredom and self-destruction." God's well-timed words have redirected my path, rescued me from temptation, and re-energized me during some of my deepest moments of despair" (p. 21). Hybels casts a vision for what life can look like when Christ's followers choose to hear from God as they navigate life on earth when they have the passion for pursuing God's promptings. He writes:

> Whispers that arbitrate key decisions, nudges that rescue from
> dark nights of the soul, promptings that spur on growth,
> urgings that come by way of another person, inspiration that

opens once-glazed-over eyes to the terrible plight people face
in this world. (p. 88)

Hybels urges people "in all walks of life, to walk obediently pursuing
the passion that a wide-open heart that has heard from God directs
them to do" (p. 48).

Bolles (2018) wrote his best-selling classic, *What Color Is Your
Parachute: A Practical Manual for Job-Hunters and Career-Changers,* in
1972. As a former Episcopalian preacher in the San Francisco area,
Bolles got laid off. He also noticed that this was a national trend and
that many pastors needed a new job due to this forced career change.
He began interviewing employers and asking them what they looked
for when hiring new people. He collected his research and his
thoughts and self-published his research findings. Before passing
away on March 31, 2017, at 90, Bolles updated and revised this book
annually. His masterpiece has sold over 10 million copies, has 40
editions, and has been translated into 20 languages. By the millions of
copies sold and the 40-year longevity of this book, one can see that
these time-tested principles for helping people discover their
purposeful place in the employment sector have been successful.
Bolles writes that one of the critical ingredients to both short-term
success and long-term fulfillment is identifying a job that one is
passionate about performing. One of Bolles's (2018) principles for

finding employment is searching for what you love, not just for what you can do. He writes that passion plus competency is the key to securing fulfilling employment, not just competency alone.

CONCLUSION

In this chapter, we examined Dr. Vallerand's Dualistic Model of Passion. In this model, he proposes two types of passion: harmonious passion, which remains under the person's control, and obsessive passion, which controls the person. While harmonious passion typically leads to adaptive behaviors, the obsessive form of passion leads to less adaptive and, at times, maladaptive behaviors.

Srikant & Sadachar (2018) note that harmonious passion refers to feeling the choice of engaging in the activity that one loves and is hypothesized to lead to more adaptive outcomes. On the other hand, obsessive passion reflects internal pressure to participate in an activity one loves. These two types of passion answer the paradox raised by philosophers on the seemingly contradictory positive and negative outcomes engendered by passion. Vallerand (2015) highlights the effects of these two types of passion on several psychological phenomena, such as cognition, emotions, performance, relationships, aggression, and violence. Vallerand (2015) concludes that passion is different from emotion. Passion can be both positive and negative. The role that passion plays in the psychology of a person is powerful.

Finally, we also reviewed a Christian perspective on passion. Hybels (2007) contends that "holy discontent occurs when one is so stirred by something (a cause, an injustice, etc.) that one simply has to do something" (p.13). He explains that one cannot go another minute, much less another day, without taking action when one is passionate about something. Hybels (2007) calls this passion. He writes that people are passionate about sports teams, jobs, social injustice, politics, clean drinking water, education, a cure for cancer, electric cars, traveling, teenagers, babies, elderly, unwed mothers in inner-city areas, social media, and even religion.

We also briefly examined Bolles (2018), who wrote his best-selling classic, *What Color Is Your Parachute: A Practical Manual for Job-Hunters and Career-Changers,* in 1972. Before passing away on March 31, 2017, at 90, Bolles updated and revised this book annually. His masterpiece has sold over 10 million copies, has 40 editions, and has been translated into 20 languages. By the millions of copies sold and the 40-year longevity of this book, one can see that these time-tested principles for helping people discover their purposeful place in the employment sector have been successful. Bolles writes that one of the critical ingredients to both short-term success and long-term fulfillment is identifying a job that one is passionate about performing.

CHAPTER SEVEN
Steps to Discovering Your Passion

So, how do you discover your passion? In this chapter, we will examine three different instruments written in three separate vocational disciplines (a pastor, a businessman, and a medical doctor) to assist you in discovering your God-given passion. There are other instruments and probing questions, but these three assessments will get you started on the right foot by asking you to reflect and introspect on how the God of the universe has uniquely designed and wired you with a passion. Bill Hybels (1990), a well-known pastor, lists five questions that help people discover their passion. These five questions are:

WHAT LOCAL, GLOBAL, POLITICAL, SOCIAL, OR CHURCH ISSUES STIR YOU EMOTIONALLY?

2 WHAT GROUP OF PEOPLE DO
YOU FEEL MOST ATTRACTED TO?

_____

_____

_____

3 WHAT AREA OF NEED IS OF
ULTIMATE IMPORTANCE TO YOU?

_____

_____

_____

4 IF YOU KNEW YOU COULD NOT
FAIL, WHAT WOULD YOU DO
WITH YOUR LIFE?

_____

_____

_____

5 WHAT AREA OF YOUR CHURCH'S
MINISTRY WOULD YOU MOST LIKE
TO INFLUENCE?

_____

_____

_____

Answering these questions can help you detect a passion for things like:

- unwed mothers
- underprivileged areas
- unbelievers
- nations with insufficient drinking water
- medical needs in specific regions of the world
- feeding those in need
- America's youth
- Discipleship
- children in foster care
- business executives

> "I HAVE NO SPECIAL TALENTS. I AM ONLY PASSIONATELY CURIOUS."
>
> **ALBERT EINSTEIN**

Many people also discover that their passion is related to their life stories. For example, growing up in a broken home may give one a passion for single parents. Likewise, growing up with a grandparent may tender one's heart to the needs of the elderly. If your youth group was vital during your teen years, then you may discover that your passion is youth ministry.

In the previously cited best-selling book, *What Color Is Your Parachute: A Practical Manual for Job-Hunters and Career-Changers* (2018), Bolles, who was a Pastor turned businessman, after writing about the importance of self-inventory, states that understanding what you are passionate about is the key to both deciding what career that you desire to pursue, and to answer the following questions about yourself before you walk into any interview:

- Why are you here?
- What can you do for us?
- What kind of person are you?
- What distinguishes you from the nineteen other people we interview for the job?
- Can we afford you?

ONE CANNOT ANSWER THESE QUESTIONS CONFIDENTLY FOR OTHERS IF THEY HAVE NOT FIRST DISCOVERED THESE ANSWERS FOR THEMSELVES.

Bolles (2018) says that one cannot answer these questions confidently for others if they have not first discovered these answers for themselves. And to answer these questions accurately, Bolles says you must know your personality type (discussed later in this book), temperament, gifts (next section), and *passion.*

Dr. Susan Biali, M.D. (2012) is a medical doctor, media health and wellness expert, life and health coach, professional speaker, and author. She has dedicated her life to helping people worldwide get healthy, find happiness, and enjoy more meaningful experiences they love. Biali references steps to determining passion. These five steps are also cited in various forms by several other physicians, psychologists, and mental health experts. Her steps to finding one's passion are:

INVENTORY YOUR TALENTS. WHAT ARE YOU GOOD AT OR HAVE AN APTITUDE FOR?

PAY ATTENTION TO WHO MAKES YOU ANNOYED OR JEALOUS. THE TRUTH BEHIND THAT ANNOYANCE IS THAT YOU MAY WISH THAT YOU COULD LIVE THAT FREELY.

THINK OF WHAT YOU LOVED TO DO AS A CHILD. BEFORE WE GROW UP, MOST OF US KNOW BEST WHO WE ARE AND WHAT MAKES US HAPPIEST.

NOTICE WHEN YOU LOSE TRACK OF TIME OR WHAT YOU HATE TO STOP DOING. WHEN YOU LOSE TRACK OF TIME, YOU ARE PROBABLY DOING SOMETHING THAT YOU LOVE.

SEE YOUR PASSION HUNT AS A FUN AND JOYFUL ADVENTURE. DON'T RUSH THE PROCESS OR BE AFRAID OF GETTING IT WRONG.

CONCLUSION

This chapter examined the steps required to help you discover your passion. We looked at three different models written from the perspective of three vocational professions – a pastor, a businessman (and author), and a medical doctor. While there are various ways to research your passion and several career-calling inventories to take, your God-ordained passion for a demographic (people group), a geographical region, or a cause is critical to you discovering God's individual vocational will for your life.

> "THE ONLY WAY TO DO GREAT WORK IS TO LOVE WHAT YOU DO."
>
> **STEVE JOBS**

CHAPTER EIGHT

Examples of Passionate Leaders

Behind all successful businesses, corporations, ministries, or causes, you will find a passionate leader. A leader who was willing to risk it all. A leader who would not take no for an answer. A leader who possesses uncommon grit, fierce determination, and unlimited energy. The literature has comprehensively proven that *passion* is the essential fuel that drives all the other character traits required to lead an organization or cause.

The Wright Brothers believed they could create an airplane that would enable people to fly, and their passion for success drove them to achieve this unimaginable feat. On December 17, 1903, at Kitty Hawk, North Carolina, the Wright Flyer became the first powered, heavier-than-air machine to achieve controlled, sustained flight with a pilot aboard. The Wright brothers created the first successful airplane, and over time would change how the world travels. They were passionate about this invention and, through trial and error, would not take "no" for an answer.

In a time in our nation's history when the horse and carriage was the predominant mode of transportation, even when developing the "western" United States, Henry Ford, using Fred Taylor's research, believed that the automobile could be built on an assembly line to make its manufacturing both more efficient and more affordable. Thus, over time, Ford's *passion* for "inventing" led him to create the assembly line process to build the automobile. This new manufacturing model enabled him to lower the time to develop an automobile from 30 days to 93 minutes. Ford's *passion* made the car more affordable to the "ordinary" person, not just the financial elite, and changed the transportation industry worldwide forever.

Walt Disney's *passion* was he dreamed of building the world's number one family-friendly vacation destination in the world based on creating a *"magical"* experience engaging one's imagination. However, "The Happiest Place on Earth" was not an easy or clear road to success. Rumor has it that the concept for one of the most visited tourist sites and theme parks in the world was turned down *over 300 times by bankers* and financiers. *Passion* drives perseverance. *Passion* maximizes your internal drive and fortitude (grit) and pushes you to overcome obstacles.

Obstacles are what we see when we take our eyes off our goal. If Walt Disney had given up, the world would not have many world-renowned theme parks, ride attractions, newly created areas of each theme park, and creative and imaginative movies and musicals that we have today. Walt changed the television, film, and tourist industries in his lifetime based on his *passion* and his refusal to accept the word "no" when he was deeply convicted about his *passion*.

One of Disney's brilliant creations behind the scenes fueling this passion is a department in the Disney corporation called Imagineering. This is the "think tank" for many of Disney's incredible new parks, attractions, and

> # OBSTACLES ARE WHAT WE SEE WHEN WE TAKE OUR EYES OFF OUR GOAL.

movies. In his book *Hatch*, a former Disney Imagineer, McNair Wilson shares the seven agreements of brainstorming, which enable those incredibly passionate about the creative processes to develop new ideas, inventions, plays, movies, or even better ways to perform "routine" tasks.

Hatch is a "must-have" for your library. If you are passionate about ministry and service in a local church, on a para-church board, or in a Christian camping ministry. I highly recommend you teach and utilize McNair's seven agreements of brainstorming in your organization. We used these seven agreements regularly to develop our themes, programming, and facilities at Carolina Creek. My favorite McNair Wilson quote from our two years of working with him (and there are a lot of them) at Carolina Creek to develop our elementary camp, the Wild (see pages 61 and 62 in *Hatch*) is, "if you are not who God created you to be, then all of creation is incomplete."

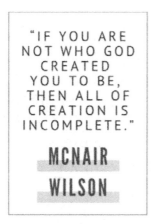

Henry Ford and Walt Disney, two of the most passionate leaders our world has ever known, shared one interesting quote in common. They both said, "people who know *how* will always work for people who know *why*." The people who know "why" are the visionaries who possess the passion and vision to overcome obstacles and persevere, regardless of their challenges.

John F. Kennedy said the United States would place a man on the moon within the decade. On May 25, 1961, President John F. Kennedy gave a historic speech before a joint session of Congress that set the United States on a course to the moon.

In his speech, Kennedy called for an ambitious space exploration program that included not just missions to put astronauts on the moon by the end of the decade and also a Rover nuclear rocket, weather satellites, and other space projects.

On July 20, 1969, Neil Armstrong became the first human to step on the moon. He and Aldrin walked around for three hours. When another aeronautical pioneer from Ohio, Neil Armstrong, became the first man to step foot on the moon in 1969, *inside his spacesuit pocket was a piece of muslin fabric from the left wing of the original 1903 Wright Flyer along with a piece of wood from the airplane's left propeller.*

Mother Teresa was passionate about the destitute and dying in the slums of Calcutta – now known as the slums of Kolkata. In 1979, she received the Nobel Peace Prize for her lifetime of passionate work serving the impoverished people in this region.

Four well-known and respected leaders in the Christian community are James Dobson, Luis Palau, John Perkins, and R.C. Sproul. These men are the founders of ministries with national and international impact for Christ. Yet, if one compares their respective ministries, one would discover that each is directed to different audiences. Each target audience of these leaders reflects their *passion*.

James Dobson, the founder of Focus on the Family ministries and the national radio program, is *passionate* about the family. Many people who interviewed Dr. Dobson claim you better have plenty of time to listen if you ask him about family. There is nothing that Dr. Dobson would have rather talked about than the family's condition, needs, value, and future. Dr. Dobson's passion is the family, and he applies all his gifts to researching and serving the family. His professional career, which includes authoring over 70 books, producing multiple films, hundreds of speaking engagements, various interviews, and his nationally produced daily radio program, is devoted to his *passion*, serving the family.

Luis Palau, the international evangelist, has a *passion* for the lost. He is driven daily by the lost condition of so many people today. Palau says, "Give me the gospel and some good music, and we'll do damage in enemy territory" (p. 23). We'll be faithful in partnership with local churches to reach metropolitan cities. Then we will corporately promote stadium events and watch God do fantastic work. Palau travels from crusade to crusade, country to country, reaching the lost, much like his predecessor, the evangelist of America, and to the Presidents of the United States for more than five decades, Billy Graham.

John Perkins, the founder of Voice of Calvary Ministries, is passionate about minorities and the inner city. He devotes his time, talent, and treasure to setting up programs to help needy people find dignity and self-esteem by developing vocational life skills and assisting them in finding meaningful employment opportunities.

R. C. Sproul, a well-respected theologian and author is passionate about studying and teaching the most profound truths of the Christian faith. He enjoys small group discussions with groups of seminarians. He likes to discuss cosmological arguments for the existence of God. As one student said of R.C. Sproul, "more than once while listening to R.C. Sproul, I have felt like the train left the station, and I was still standing on the platform."

Jerry Laymon Falwell, Sr., was an American Baptist pastor, televangelist, and conservative activist. He was the founding pastor of the Thomas Road Baptist Church, a megachurch in Lynchburg, Virginia. He founded Lynchburg Christian Academy (now Liberty Christian Academy) in 1967, founded Liberty University in 1971, and co-founded the Moral Majority in 1979. As a passionate pastor, teacher, and visionary, he desired to "train Champions for Christ" and transform his family farm into the world's largest Christian university that could offer a wide variety of undergraduate and graduate degrees that could compete academically and athletically with the largest institutions of higher education in the United States and around the world. Falwell's *passion*, faith, determination, and leadership enabled him to succeed in this endeavor, and today Liberty University is the world's largest Christian University.

Ron Blue, Dave Ramsey, and Larry Burkett are three nationally and internationally known financial experts who share a *passion* for helping people incorporate wise budgeting principles into their lives. These men regularly speak on radio broadcasts, at events, conduct workshops, and produce multiple media products, including videos, TED Talks, YouTube channel videos, and social media recommendations to assist individuals, couples, businesses, and corporations. Helping people avoid debt, get out of debt, and produce long-term financial stability and wealth motivates them to use their passion and gifts to meet the financial needs of others.

John Maxwell is *passionate* about leadership. He has become the leading voice regarding leadership in this generation. He completed his bachelor's degree at Circleville Bible College, his Master of

Divinity degree at Azusa Pacific University, and a Doctor of Ministry at Fuller Theological Seminary.

Maxwell is a leadership expert, speaker, and author. He founded INJOY, Maximum Impact, The John Maxwell Team, ISS, and EQUIP. EQUIP is an international leadership development organization working to help leaders, involved with leaders from more than 80 nations. Its mission is "to see effective Christian leaders fulfill the Great Commission in every nation."

Maxwell speaks annually to *Fortune 500* companies, international government leaders, and organizations as diverse as the United States Military Academy at West Point and the National Football League. A *New York Times*, *Wall Street Journal*, and *Business Week* best-selling author, he was among 25 authors named to Amazon.com's 10th Anniversary Hall of Fame. Three of his books, *The 21 Irrefutable Laws of Leadership*, *Developing the Leader Within You*, and *21 Indispensable Qualities of a Leader*, have sold over a million copies *each*. His *passion* is leadership, and his prolonged unquenchable thirst for its principles and practices are unrivaled.

Elisabeth Elliot was a missionary and a critically acclaimed author and speaker. For over half a century, her life of obedience, timeless teachings, and best-selling books have influenced believers and seekers of the Christian faith. The resounding theme of Elliot's life, and her *passion*, was the boundless love of Jesus, and her greatest commission was to tell others of His saving grace. This costly *passion* led her into the Amazonian jungle of Ecuador, where her husband, Jim Elliot, was one of five missionaries speared to death in 1956 while attempting to make contact with members of the Auca/Waodani tribe. Elisabeth and her young daughter Valerie would later return to Auca territory to live among and minister to the people who killed her husband. Familiar with suffering, Elliot wrote, "The deepest things that I have learned in my own life have come from the deepest suffering. And out of the deepest waters and the hottest fires have come the deepest things I know about God."

> WHEN YOU LOOK AT THE OAK TREE, YOU DON'T FEEL THAT THE LOSS' OF THE ACORN IS A VERY GREAT LOSS. THE MORE YOU PERCEIVE GOD'S PURPOSE IN YOUR LIFE, THE LESS TERRIBLE THE LOSSES SEEM."
>
> **ELISABETH ELLIOT**

Another example of a powerful moment of *passion* that led to several influential men receiving and confirming their passionate call to serve God and create world-changing ministries occurred at Forest Home Christian Camps led by Dr. Henrietta Mears. This moment happened when Dr. Henrietta Mears held a retreat, and several passionate men would describe God's presence and revelation as something that only God could do. One of those men was struggling to walk in his vocational calling, but Billy Graham would describe this as the life-changing event that God used to solidify his *passion* for walking courageously in his calling to be an evangelist. Today at Forest Home, there is even a memorial stone to mark this event at this location, much like the Israelites of the Old Testament would build a pile of rocks to mark a place where God had shown up in a remarkable way. Graham would later write,

> "Dr. Henrietta C. Mears has had a remarkable influence, both directly and indirectly, on my life. In fact, I doubt any other woman outside my wife and mother has had such a marked influence. She is certainly one of the greatest Christians I have ever known!"

Also in attendance at this same dynamic retreat was Bill Bright, the founder of Campus Crusade for Christ (now CRU) and author of the Four Spiritual Laws, and Jim Rayburn, the founder of Young Life, who confirmed their passion for beginning these powerful ministries that are still passionately changing lives today.

> "YOU TEACH A LITTLE BY WHAT YOU SAY. YOU TEACH MOST BY WHAT YOU ARE."
>
> HENRIETTA MEARS

No list of passionate Christian leaders would be complete without including singer, songwriter, and performer Chris Tomlin and nationally known speaker, preacher, author, and leader Louie Giglio. Tomlin's incredible talent and gifting in the music industry are "indescribable," as one of his songs about God's universe accurately records. Similarly, Giglio has been widely regarded as one of the most influential and sought-after speakers and leaders to the "emerging adults" generation, aged 18-25, for over a decade. Giglio and Tomlin's annual event of the largest group of college and young adults worldwide each December or January that attracts famous artists, performers, and speakers is even called "*Passion*."

But, as listed previously, many passionate people also pursue non-evangelical causes. A story that always encourages me personally is the story of Teach For America. During her senior year at Princeton University, Wendy Kopp was trying to figure out what she wanted to do when she graduated. She was not even considering starting her own business or non-profit. Throughout her time at Princeton, Kopp had noticed two distinct and divergent camps of students, even within that elite institution. One group of students had attended top-flight East Coast prep schools. These students referred to their time at Princeton as a cakewalk. The other group consisted of students who had grown up in urban public schools and struggled mightily at this Ivy League institution.

Kopp gathered a group of students to discuss the reasons for this wide educational gap. Instead of hearing about the inadequate educational facilities, lack of teacher pay, homelessness, and the alarming crime statistics that she anticipated, in this focus group, she heard student after student say that they wish that they could be a part of the low educational community solution, but that there was no mechanism or organization mobilized to attract these types of elite students to serve in these impoverished areas.

This was the day that Kopp discovered her *passion*. Based on President John K. Kennedy's Peace Corps model, Kopp was determined to create a national teacher corps. She raised 2.5 million dollars in her first year, recruited, and interviewed 2,500 applicants, hired 500 first-year elite-level teachers, organized the first training orientation at the University of Southern California, and Teach for America was born. Wendy Kopp's *passion* for getting quality teachers into the urban inner-city parts of America has transformed thousands of lives. Today Teach for America is providing teachers and helping overcome massive deficits in over 50 urban inner-city communities.

What if one attempted to change the places of any of these previously mentioned leaders? Could Dr. James Dobson organize and preach at international crusades? Could R.C. Sproul have started Teach for America? What separates these talented and dynamic leaders? The answer is *passion*. Each of these leaders displays a *passion* that drives a tireless work ethic, a sacrificial leadership and management style, and an unquenchable thirst to be a part of the solution for a problem in our world.

I would also mention that passion can fuel "eternal significance" outside of a person's *primary* vocational field. For example, as the founding Executive Director of Carolina Creek Christian Camps, we had numerous donors and Board members who were overwhelmingly successful entrepreneurs in home building, oil and gas, financial planning, technology, software and website development, banking, medicine, and law.

These men and women were *passionate* about each of their "primary" vocations and very successful. As Buford would write in his book, *Halftime*, they had moved from "success to significance." In addition to creating companies and generating generational wealth, they served faithfully on Boards. They made generous financial contributions to many hospitals, museums, churches, para-church organizations, and Christian camping ministries, because of their *passion* for helping and serving others (hospitals and museums) and allowing others to hear the truths of the Bible and have opportunities to experience the life-transforming difference that a relationship with Jesus Christ and make in people's lives. So, while *passion* is discussed in this book as a necessary "compass" directing one's vocational life, *passion* can also be a significant driver in someone's life outside of their primary vocation to enrich and enhance the lives of others.

In the world of elite sports, the chart beside depicts some of the world's most well-known athletes and coaches that are widely regarded as among the best ever to play or coach their sport at the highest level.

ACCOMPLISHMENTS

TOM BRADY NFL Quarterback, Seven-Time Super Bowl Champion

JOE MONTANA Four-Time NFL Champion

TERRY BRADSHAW Four-Time NFL Champion

PAYTON MANNING NFL Quarterback, Two-Time Super Bowl Champion

MICHAEL JORDAN Six-Time NBA Champion

STEPH CURRY Four-Time NBA Champion, All-Time Three Point Shot Leader

LEBRON JAMES Three-Time NBA Champion, All-Time Scoring Leader

KOBE BRYANT Three-Time NBA Champion

BABE RUTH 714 Home Runs, Seven-Time MLB Champion

GREG MADDUX Pitcher, 355 Wins, Most All-Time

WAYNE GRETZKY Four-Time Stanley Cup Winner, Most Goals, Assists, Points, All-Time

MICHAEL PHELPS Olympic Swimmer, 23 Gold Medals, 28 Overall

KATIE LEDECKY Olympic Swimmer, Ten-Time Olympic Medalist, 10 Gold, 3 Silver

CARL LEWIS Ten-Time Olympic Medalist, 9 Gold, and 1 Silver

SIMONE BILES Seven-Time Olympic Medalist, 25 World Championship Medals (most ever)

SERENA WILLIAMS Greatest Women's Tennis Player of All Time, Won 23 Majors

MIA HAMM Two-Time Olympic Gold Medalist and World Cup Champion

VINCE LOMBARDI Won 5 NFL Championships Overall Record 96-34-6, Playoffs 9-1

BILL BELICHICK Won 6 Super Bowl Titles, Most All-Time

DON SHULA All-Time Winningest NFL Coach, 347 Wins

JOHN WOODEN Won Ten NCAA Basketball Championships at UCLA, Nine in a Row

NICK SABAN Seven-Time NCAA Championship Head Football Coach

When you study the information about these athletes in books, magazine articles, newspapers, and personal interviews, you can quickly identify one thing they ALL have in common – *passion*. When asked, "What was the one force that drove each of them to these unprecedented accomplishments?" they would tell you it is *passion*. God-given ability alone does not create the greatest of all time in sports. It requires hours of perfecting their skills, and these hours are driven by a *passion* for being the very best. As Steph Curry says, "I've always been a believer that the Lord has put whatever talent in you, and whatever gift He has put in you, He wants you to get the most out of that. He wants you to succeed. He wants you to pursue and work and be *passionate* about it." Passion drives these elite athletes to unprecedented heights. *Passion* pushes elite athletes to get up earlier, train harder, study longer, and never be "satisfied." Passion is what makes Tom Brady never satisfied. Passion makes Simone Biles add more difficulty to all four gymnastic routines when she is already the best female gymnast the world has ever seen. Passion brings Michael Phelps and Katie Ledecky back to the pool at 5:00 am every day when they are already the most accomplished and decorated Olympic medal-winning swimmers ever.

> "FAILING TO PREPARE IS PREPARING TO FAIL."
>
> JOHN WOODEN

As we close our discussion on passion, it should also be noted, unfortunately, that not all passion is a positive driving force of success, changing the world, or giving sacrificially for the good of others. Passion can also be negative or excruciating. One of the most well-known examples of this may be Mel Gibson's movie, the *Passion of Christ*. While the results of Christ's passion would bring salvation to all who believe in the life, death, burial, and resurrection of Jesus Christ, for Jesus, his *passion,* as portrayed in this powerful film, was the passion for withstanding such agony and torture that he did not deserve on behalf of humanity that He came to save. So, while the results of Christ's *passion* were overwhelmingly positive for humanity, the cost for Jesus was his very life. But He was passionate about returning all of humanity to His Heavenly Father and providing a pathway for us to choose to accept the free gift of salvation.

Another way to see passion lived out negatively for a person but positively for someone else is when a passionate person is willing to make a sacrificial gift like bone marrow or a kidney for a child, loved one, close friend, or maybe even a stranger to be able to live. While this is an incredible act of kindness and usually results from a passion for helping another life, it is the most difficult and painful process for the donor. I am reminded of the little girl who was willing to give a blood transfusion to her mother because she was a blood donor match. When the little girl woke up, she was confused because she did not understand that she would live after the surgery. Being very young, she misunderstood the details of the procedure before the surgery, and she thought that the transfusion meant that she would die, but she loved her mother so much and wanted her mother to live for her Daddy and her siblings, so she was willing to do it.

In another negative context, passion can lead people to make poor decisions to commit crimes, harm others, place harmful chemicals in their bodies, harm themselves, and even perform acts of violence toward others. Many crimes and gang-related violence can be traced back to people so passionate about belonging to a particular group that they will commit acts of violence to someone (usually a stranger) that they would never perform on their own. So, while passion overall is widely considered a positive, life-giving, energetic, and enthusiastic driver of human behavior, it should be noted that passion can also occasionally be used in a harmful and hurtful way.

CONCLUSION

What do the Wright Brothers, Henry Ford, Walt Disney, John F. Kennedy, Mother Teresa, James Dobson, John Maxwell, Tom Brady, Steph Curry, and Simone Biles all have in common? *Passion*. The first step of the three-step practical model for discovering God's individual vocational will for your life is to take the time necessary to find your God-ordained *passion* by answering the questions provided in these last two chapters and spending the time required for self-discovery to discern how God has created you and given you a *passion* for, a particular people group, a geographic location, or a cause.

Until you can accurately discover and discern your God-ordained *passion*, you will struggle to find God's ordained vocational will for your life. As we discovered, passion drives people to work harder and longer with an increased physical and mental capacity than others because their passion drives them to overcome obstacles and challenges in the face of adversity. Passionate people will study harder, research more diligently, practice longer, and refuse to quit when non-passionate people give up.

In the shaded oval, write the word "Passion." Taking the time to discover your passion is step one in completing the three-step model.

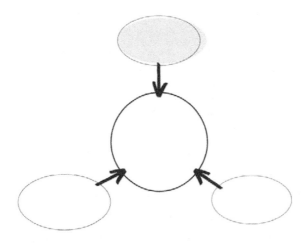

DISCERNING GOD'S INDIVIDUAL VOCATIONAL WILL
THE OGLESBY MODEL

SECTION THREE

SPIRITUAL GIFTS

The second element of you discovering your individual vocational will for your life is understanding how God uniquely fashioned you with a spiritual gift. I hope the following sections will broaden your understanding of spiritual gifts, including a brief but detailed explanation of how people today see spiritual gifts, their origin, and their purpose in our world. An important place to start this discussion is to ask, "Where did spiritual gifts come from, and what is their purpose?"

In Ephesians 4:7-8, the Apostle Paul gives us a beautiful word picture. But to each one of us grace has been given as Christ apportioned it. This is why it says: "When he ascended on high, he led captivity captive, and gave gifts unto men."

In Gill's Commentary, he dissects this imagery for us. I will provide a brief overview here but a more detailed explanation in chapter ten that follows. In summary, when Jesus ascended on high (back to heaven) after his resurrection, he took "captivity captive." This means that in His resurrection, Jesus took sin, death, the grave, Satan, and every form of the spiritual enemy, including the devils' s principalities and powers who hold men "captive" into "captivity" for all time both here on earth and in eternity! Can I get an "Amen!" Gill writes that the allusion here is to the public triumphs of the Romans, in which captives were led in chains and exposed to open public humiliation. This is what Christ did to Satan at the resurrection!

But Paul's description in this one powerful verse gets even better! Jesus took "captivity captive," and in His victory, He also gave gifts unto men." Thus, when Jesus ascended after His resurrection and having taken Satan captive, He gave gifts (spiritual gifts) unto men as a reward for this victory and to use these gifts to continue to proclaim His victory over sin and death to others until He returns. So, going back to Paul's writing and the original passage and imagery, it was customary at triumphs for the leader to bestow gifts to his soldiers who were responsible for the Victory to honor them. Therefore, when Jesus took captivity captive (and defeated Satan for good), He also gave us spiritual gifts to proclaim His victory to others while we are here until He returns.

Later in this same passage, in Ephesians 4:11-13, Paul gives us one of the four passages in scripture that outline these gifts:

> So Christ himself gave some to be the apostles, some to be prophets, some to be evangelists, and some to be pastors and teachers, to equip his people for works of service, so that the body of Christ may be built up until we all reach unity in the faith and in the knowledge of the Son of God and become mature, attaining to the whole measure of the fullness of Christ. (Ephesians 4:11-13)

In the following chapter, I will expand on these verses in Ephesians in more detail. Also, as you will discover in the following chapters, everyone must prayerfully ask God through the indwelling of His Holy Spirit for their own understanding and interpretation of the distribution, use, and meaning of spiritual gifts in the Bible. This is a widely debated area of theology. While I conclude after extensive prayer, research, Bible study, and comparative analysis of various commentaries that everyone has a spiritual gift (1 Cor. 12:1) and will be held accountable for utilizing their gift while here on earth, I do provide you with other well-documented perspectives for you to prayerfully consider as well.

CHAPTER NINE

What is a Spiritual Gift?

The second step in this practical three-step model is for one to discern their spiritual gift. A surprising number of believers who have heard the term spiritual gifts are unsure what their gifts are. There are even those who feel, for some reason, they have been left out and do not have a spiritual gift (Wagner, 2012). Teaching spiritual gifts is a prominent topic in the New Testament. The apostle Paul says to the believers in the church in Corinth, "Now concerning spiritual gifts, brethren, I do not want you to be ignorant" (1 Corinthians 12:1). Furthermore, if one does not know their spiritual gift, they may well be missing out on God's best plan for their lives (Schreiner, 2018).

Piper (2010) states that if one is a born-again believer and a member of the body of Christ, one possesses one or more spiritual gifts. The goal of discerning God's individual vocational will for your life is to identify your spiritual gift accurately and then understand how to use it for your God-ordained purpose - to encourage the saints and build the Kingdom (Schreiner, 2018). In fact, perhaps you may even realize that you have been using one or more of your spiritual gifts without even knowing it (Wagner, 2012).

SPIRITUAL GIFTS: A HISTORICAL PERSPECTIVE

What does the term 'spiritual gift' mean? The answer to this question depends considerably on who one asks. For W. R. Jones to judge by the title and contents of his essay in a handbook of Pentecostal doctrine, there are just nine gifts (Brewster, 1976). They are set out in 1 Corinthians 12:8-10 as words of wisdom, words of knowledge, discerning of spirits, 'faith,' working of miracles, gifts of healing, prophecy, tongues, and interpretation), and Jones would readily point you to phenomena in his church which (he would claim) (Turner, 1985) were denotata of these nine specified gifts (Hurford & Hensley, 1977).

At the other end of the spectrum, we find writers who give such a broad sense to the expressions of spiritual gifts, or charismata, that it is barely possible to think of any event which belongs properly (*nota bene*) to the life of the Christian who could not legitimately be called a denotatum of the terms. Käsemann's (1969) essay on ministry in the early church tends in this direction. Besides Kasemann (1969), we may also note the position of Rahner (1979) and Dussel (1978). For them, the charisms of the Spirit cannot be exhausted within the confines of the church (Turner, 1985). According to these two authors, any existential grace experience is an experience and gift of the Spirit (Laurentin, 1978).

So, one has a problem: what exactly are we talking about when we speak of spiritual gifts? The answer to this question is one that several twentieth-century writers have wrestled with throughout the ages. Many of these authors give various semantic extensions to the expression of spiritual gifts. The problem is not merely one of defining extension, but at the root of that difficulty is the problem of giving what is called a semantic stereotype of spiritual gifts (Turner, 1985).

Can one avoid the problem of defining a spiritual gift by examining the question back at its origin? What exactly did the New Testament writers mean by the term spiritual gifts? This looks like a viable solution at first, but upon closer examination, we find this has problems. The fact is that Paul and Luke, even if they used the same terminology as each other, are not native speakers of English and do not use the phrase spiritual gifts at all. So, the term spiritual gifts were loosely defined until the term reemerged in the 1970s. Wagner (2012) writes that a relatively new thing happened to the church of Jesus Christ in America during the 1970s. The third person of the Trinity began to come into His own in the understanding of those using the term. The Holy Spirit has always been present. In fact, creeds, hymns, and liturgies have attested to the central place of the Holy Spirit in the Orthodoxy of the Christian faith. Systematic theologies throughout the centuries have included sections on pneumatology, affirming the Holy Spirit's position in Christian thought (Wagner, 2012).

But rarely in the church's history has there been such an enormous desire to move beyond the creeds and theologies to a personal experience of the Holy Spirit in the everyday life of the church the way that we are witnessing it today. As a result, one of the most emerging facets of this new experience of the Holy Spirit is the rediscovery of one's spiritual gift (Wagner, 2012). Why does Wagner (2012) say rediscovery?

It is reasonably easy to fix the date when this new interest in spiritual gifts began. The production of literature itself is a sufficiently accurate indicator. "A decent seminary library may catalog forty or fifty books on spiritual gifts" (Wagner, 2012, p. 9). Probably more than ninety percent of them would have been written after 1970. Previous to 1970, a seminary graduate characteristically left their institution knowing little or nothing about spiritual gifts. The American church was genuinely ignorant of spiritual gifts. Today, almost all seminaries and Bible colleges include teaching spiritual gifts as a regular part of their curriculum (Schreiner, 2018).

The roots, however, of this newfound fascination with spiritual gifts trace back to 1900. This is the most widely accepted day for what is known as the classical Pentecostal movement. During a watch-night service beginning on December 31, 1900, on the first day of the twentieth century, Charles Parham of Topeka, Kansas, laid his hands on Agnes Ozman. She began speaking in tongues, and the movement had officially started. This started a fascinating series of events that triggered the famous Los Angeles Azusa Street Revival. This revival began in 1906 under the ministry of William Seymour, and with that, the Pentecostal movement gained high visibility and momentum that has never been relented (Wagner, 2012).

The original intent of the Pentecostal leaders was to influence the significant Christian denominations from within, reminiscent of the early intentions of such leaders as Martin Luther and John Wesley. But just as Lutheranism was incompatible with the Catholic church in the sixteenth century and Methodism was incompatible with the Anglican Church in the eighteenth century, Pentecostalism found itself incompatible with the mainline denominations in the twentieth century.

Thus, as others had done before them, Pentecostal leaders reluctantly found it necessary to establish a new denomination where they could develop a lifestyle directly under the influence of the Holy Spirit and an atmosphere of freedom and mutual support. Such denominations we know today as Assemblies of God, Pentecostal Holiness, Church of God in Christ, Church of the four square Gospel, Church of God Cleveland Tennessee, and many others were formed for that purpose (Piper, 2010).

Phase two of this movement started after World War II when Pentecostal leaders again attempted to join the mainstream. The beginnings were slow. Some Pentecostal denominations began gaining social respect by affiliating with organizations such as the National Association of Evangelicals (Wagner, 2012). Consequently, they began to neutralize the opinion that Pentecostalism was a false cult to be placed alongside the Jehovah's Witnesses, the Mormons, or the spiritualist.

Finally, in 1970, the independent charismatic movement built freestanding charismatic churches separate from mainstream denominations. For the next 25 years, these independent charismatic churches were the fastest-growing churches in the United States (Schreiner, 2018).

THE DEMISE OF CESSATIONISM

Not everyone, however, agrees with this newfound arrival of spiritual gifts. Some, for example, argue that many of the gifts went out of use after the lives of the apostles. The epicenter of this belief is found at the Dallas Theological Seminary, an interdenominational seminary that has looked with strong opposition to the Pentecostal/charismatic movement in recent decades (Wagner, 2012). John Walvoord, the former president of Dallas Theological Seminary, feels that the miracles were granted to acknowledge the Holy Spirit's arrival in Acts and authenticate the ministry of the disciples. One of his colleagues, Merrill Unger, makes reference to Benjamin B Warfield of Princeton Seminary, who, in 1918, wrote a book called *Miracles: Yesterday and Today, True and False.* Unger says, "Other than the *Scofield Reference Bible,* it has been the most influential book written in America against the validity of the charismatic gifts today" (Wagner, 2017, p. 12). Warfield (1965) argues that these gifts were distinctively the authentication of the Apostles and passed away when they did. Warfield (1965) writes that the spiritual gifts' function was confined distinctively to the Apostolic Church, and they passed away with it (Warfield, 1965).

This notion that the more spectacular spiritual gifts ceased to exist with the apostolic age is commonly known as cessationism. Therefore, the charismatic gifts of the Holy Spirit have been only recognized by relatively small segments of the church throughout church history. But cessationism has been the prevailing thought in church doctrine. It was taught exclusively in seminaries, even in the 1950s.

However, today on a global scale, including many of the mainline denominations in the United States, many church leaders would believe that cessationism now belongs on some "endangered species doctrine" lists and that the tendency today is definitely in the direction of expecting spiritual gifts to be as operative today as they were in the first century (Wagner, 2012). So, having reviewed the historical perspective of spiritual gifts and their emphasis, de-emphasis, or even denial of their current existence over time, in the next chapter, I would like to provide you with a broad-stroke biblical foundation regarding spiritual gifts.

CONCLUSION

Spiritual gifts are one of theology's most talked about, least understood, and widely debated issues. In this chapter, I summarized my exhaustive investigation of this topic over the last four years. Feel free to view my full dissertation study in the Jerry Falwell Library at Liberty University for a complete discussion. It is also a free download from Scholars Crossing, just Google my name and Discerning God's Individual Vocational Will for One's Life.

The summary provided in this chapter defines spiritual gifts, discusses the historical perspective of spiritual gifts, and various examples of leaders and their particular views regarding spiritual gifts. Wagner's research and perspective are probably the most well-rounded, non-denominational, and objective examination of spiritual gifts and the rise and fall of the theory of Cessationism.

Of course, volumes of books, commentaries, and dissertations are written regarding spiritual gifts, their existence, and their use. I encourage you to perform your own prayerful examination of the scriptures and ask God through his incredible Holy Spirit to direct you in properly understanding this valuable and necessary part of your spiritual growth and use of your gifts to bring Him glory.

CHAPTER TEN

Spiritual Gifts:
A Biblical Perspective

If you believe that God has an individual vocational will for your life, then you must understand that taking the time to discover your spiritual gift is an essential and non-negotiable part of the process. "Spiritual gifts are the unique abilities God places in each believer at the moment of salvation, enabling one to build up and encourage other believers in the church" (Hybels, 1990, p. 111).

To understand and fully appreciate scripture and properly apply it to our life, we must study scripture in the proper context. This means knowing who wrote the book, who the audience was when it was written, what the events were taking place, what was the author's purpose, what God was telling this original audience, and what it is still telling us today in the passage. We call this inductive Bible study.

When we conduct an inductive Bible study on spiritual gifts (as briefly referenced in the introduction to spiritual gifts previously), we discover that the Apostle Paul wrote the origin of spiritual gifts in his letter to the Ephesians. Paul knew this audience well because he lived in Ephesus and led this congregation for two years while living with Pricilla and Aquila and working as a tent maker. In this letter to the Ephesians 4:7-8, written later after his tenure there, I like the King James version and the way that John Gill's Commentary describes the arrival and the purpose of spiritual gifts below:

EPHESIANS 4:7

But unto everyone of us is given grace

Which may refer to the saints in common and may be interpreted of justifying, pardoning, adopting, sanctifying, and persevering grace, bestowed upon them all, freely and liberally, not grudgingly, nor niggardly, and without motive and condition in them; or to the ministers of the Gospel, and so design gifts fitting for the ministry, which everyone has, though differing one from another, and all of free grace:

according to the measure of the gift of Christ:

either according to the gift of grace to Christ before the world began, and the measure of it, which he communicates to them in time, even grace for grace; or according to that measure of gifts which Christ received from men at his ascension: it may be observed that every member of Christ, and minister of his, receive more or less grace and gifts from him; and that what they receive is all of free grace, and in measure; and though they may have gifts differing one from another, yet all are useful; so that there is no room for pride, envy, and contempt, which would break in upon the unity of the Spirit; for what is said from (Ephesians 4:3) contains so many arguments to stir up the saints to endeavor to preserve that.

EPHESIANS 4:8

Wherefore he saith

God in the Scripture, (Psalms 68:18)

when he ascended up on high;

which is not to be understood of Moses's ascending up to the firmament at the giving of the law, as some Jewish writers interpret it; for though Moses ascended to the top of Mount Sinai, yet it is never said that he went up to the firmament of heaven; nor of David's going up to the high fortresses of his enemies, as another of those writers would have it; nor of God's ascent from Mount Sinai, when he gave the law, of which there is no mention in Scripture; but of the Messiah's ascension to heaven, which may very well be signified by this phrase, "on high"; see (Psalms 102:19) (Jeremiah 25:30) , and which ascension is to be taken not in a figurative, but literal sense, and as real, local, and visible, as Christ's ascension to heaven was; being from Mount Olivet, attended by angels, in the sight of his apostles, after he had conversed with them from the time of his resurrection forty days; and which ascension of his was in order to fulfil the type of the high priest entering into the most holy place; and to make intercession for his people, and to send down the Spirit with his gifts and graces to them, and to make way and prepare mansions of glory for them, and receive the glory promised and due to him: in the Hebrew text it is, "thou hast ascended"; there the psalmist speaks to the Messiah, here the apostle speaks of him; though the Arabic and Ethiopic read there, "he ascended", as here:

he led captivity captive;

which is expressive of Christ's conquests and triumph over sin, Satan, the world, death, and the grave; and indeed, every spiritual enemy of his and his people, especially the devil, who leads men captive at his will, and is therefore called captivity, and his principalities and powers, whom Christ has spoiled and triumphed over; the allusion is to the public triumphs of the Romans, in which captives were led in chains, and exposed to open view:

and gave gifts unto men;

meaning the gifts of the Holy Ghost, and particularly such as qualify men for the work of the ministry; these he received (Mdab) , "in man"; in human nature, in that nature in which he ascended to heaven; (hleml ewdyh Mdab) , "in the man that is known above," as say the Jews; and these he bestows on men, even rebellious ones, that the Lord God might dwell among them, and make them useful to others:

wherefore the Jews have no reason to quarrel with the version of the apostle as they do; who, instead of "received gifts for" men, renders it, "gave gifts to men"; since the Messiah received in order to give, and gives in consequence of his having received them; and so Jarchi interprets the words, (Mttl), "to give them" to the children of men; and besides, as a learned man has observed, one and the same Hebrew word signifies to give and to receive; to which may be added that their own Targum renders it (atbhy) , "and hast given gifts to the children of men"; and in like manner the Syriac and Arabic versions of (Psalms 68:18) render the words; very likely the apostle might use the Syriac version, which is a very ancient one: it was customary at triumphs to give gifts to the soldiers, to which there is an allusion here.

So, in short, the imagery provided in Gill's Commentary here describes vividly that when Jesus ascended back into heaven after His resurrection, he took "captive" death, the grave, sin, Satan, Satan's principalities and power, and every spiritual enemy of His people. And, in *Christ's victory* over sin and death, upon His ascension back to heaven, he *"gave spiritual gifts"* for us to use to share the news of His Victory with others until he returns. In Biblical times, the one who led the fight and delivered the victory was rewarded with gifts from the King. In the same way, Jesus took our sin and delivered "victory" over Satan and the sin of separation for all of humanity. "He who had no

sin, became sin so that we could become the righteousness of God."
Then, Jesus, the Victor, distributed spiritual gifts to us, his army, to
use because we will be in a battle against the fiery darts of the evil
one until He returns (which is why later in Ephesians, Paul gives us
the "full Armor of God" in Ephesians 6:10-18.). Jesus won the *victory* in
His resurrection and gave us *spiritual gifts* at His ascension to use for
His glory until His return.

A few short verses later, Paul would give one of the four passages that
list some of these spiritual gifts when he writes in Ephesian 4:11-13,

"So Christ himself gave some to be the apostles, some to be
prophets, some to be evangelists, and some to be pastors and
teachers, to equip his people for works of service, so that the
body of Christ may be built up until we all reach unity in the
faith and in the knowledge of the Son of God and become
mature, attaining to the whole measure of the fullness of
Christ."

Four primary Biblical texts teach about spiritual gifts. These passages
include:
- 1 Corinthians 12-14
- Romans 12:1-8
- Ephesians 4:1-16
- 1 Peter 4:8-11.

For simplification, Hybels (1990) divides these gifts into four broad categories. These categories are:

1) **Speaking gifts** - prophecy, teaching
2) **People-intensive gifts** - counseling, creative communications, encouragement, evangelism, hospitality, leadership, mercy, and shepherding
3) **Service gifts** - administration, craftsmanship, giving, and helps
4) **Support gifts** - apostleship, discernment, faith, healing, interpretation, knowledge, miracles, tongues, and wisdom.

Peter Wagner (2012), who authored more than 70 books, founded the Wagner Leadership Institute and possessed graduate degrees in theology, missiology, and religion from Fuller Theological Seminary, Princeton Theological Seminary, and the University of Southern California, served as a field missionary for 16 years. He taught on the Fuller School of Intercultural Studies faculty for 30 years.

For almost four decades, Wagner (2012) has been a leading voice in discovering one's spiritual gifts. His two bestselling works regarding spiritual gifts are *Discovering Your Spiritual Gifts* and *Finding Your Gifts*. These two resources have been helping believers across denominations discover their spiritual gifts. As one who has performed an exhaustive research study concerning spiritual gifts, I highly recommend Wagner's 135-question questionnaire instrument. It is very simple to complete and score. It will help you find which, and how many, and even a few blends, of God's twenty-five spiritual gifts that you have.

SPIRITUAL GIFTS

ROMANS 12:6-8

- Prophecy (preaching, inspired utterance)
- Service (ministry)
- Teaching
- Exhortation (stimulating faith, encouragement)
- Giving (contributing, generosity, sharing)
- Leadership (authority, ruling)
- Mercy (sympathy, comfort to the sorrowing, showing kindness)

EPHESIANS 4:11

- Evangelist
- Pastor (caring for God's people)

FIVE OTHER SPIRITUAL GIFTS MENTIONED IN THE NEW TESTAMENT

- Celibacy (continence – 1 Corinthians 7:7)
- Voluntary poverty (1 Corinthians 13:3)
- Martyrdom (1 Corinthians 13:3)
- Missionary (Ephesians 3:6-8)
- Hospitality (1 Peter 4:9)

1 CORINTHIANS 12:8-10

- Faith
- Healing
- Miracles
- Apostle
- Helps
- Wisdom (wise advice, wise speech)
- Knowledge (studying, speaking with knowledge)
- Discerning of spirits (discrimination in spiritual matters)
- Tongues (speaking in languages never learned)
- Interpretation of tongues
- Administration (governments, getting others to work together)

In addition, Wagner provides a complete list of these twenty-five gifts with a comprehensive definition and scripture references to help one understand what each gift means and how it works, shows a biblical and modern-day example of those who share these gifts and reveal practical and straightforward ways to use one's spiritual gift to serve God and others better (see above). As Wagner (2012) concludes, when one knows and understands the spiritual gifts that God has entrusted to them, one will discover a renewed sense of purpose and excitement as one partners with God to bless others. The chart below contains Wagner's listing of spiritual gifts.

Another perspective on discovering your spiritual gift is offered by the noted author and pastor Gene Getz, the founder of Fellowship Bible Church in Dallas, Texas. In Getz's (1974) book, *Sharpening the Focus of the Church*, Getz's perspective on the place of spiritual gifts in the functioning body of Christ is summarized when he writes that instead of a person taking a personal "paper and pencil" inventory and spiritual gifts assessment (or even electronically today), you may *experientially discover your spiritual gift* by serving the needs of others in the local church, in parachurch ministries, or on the mission field. In Getz's (1976) work, he discusses spiritual gifts within the context of the 100 - one another - imperatives that he argues are more important for the proper functioning of the local church than spiritual gifts. Getz's (1974, 1976) perspective on spiritual gifts is heavily influenced by his former professor at Dallas Theological Seminary, Dwight Pentecost. Pentecost (1970) wrote that Christians are not to seek their spiritual gifts because the distribution of gifts is based upon the sovereign decision of the Holy Spirit, as Paul taught. Based on Pentecost's (1970) influence, Getz (1976) further writes, "it suddenly dawned on me one day that nowhere in I Corinthians 12, Romans 12, or Ephesians 4 can we find any exhortation for individual Christians to 'look for' or to 'try to discover' their spiritual gift or gifts" (p. 9). Wagner (2012), however, would argue with Getz (1976) and Pentecost (1970) that while the position "we are not told anywhere in scripture to discover our gifts" may be literally true, Wagner believes that it is difficult to fully implement I Peter 4:10 into one's life without knowing how one is gifted. Wagner (2012) continues, in the context of having love for one another, Peter writes:

> As each one has received a gift, minister it to one another, as good stewards of the manifold grace of God. Like good stewards of the manifold grace of God, serve one another with whatever gift each of you has received. As each one has received a special gift, employ it in serving one another, as good stewards of the manifold grace of God. (1 Peter 4:10)

Peter could have written "serve one another," but instead, Peter adds the admonition that this service *should be according to one's gifting.* Peter's specific word choice implies a more directed and focused service than merely serving, and *it is specifically focused on the area of one's gift (charisma).* In his expositional commentary on I Peter, Hiebert (1984) writes, "According as (*kathos*), 'just as,' indicates that the service of each one is determined and is to be governed by the nature of the gift received" (p. 259).

Wagner (2012) concludes that one does not fulfill I Peter 4:10 just by serving; one fulfills it by serving "according to one's gifting," which is difficult to do if one does not know what their "gifting" is. Without this knowledge, some people will naturally seek more suitable service areas, and most churches implement gifts far more than others.

SPIRITUAL GIFTS: ONE IS ACCOUNTABLE

Finally, the Apostle Paul also reminds us that we need to take the discovery and the utilization of the spiritual gifts entrusted to us seriously. To Timothy, Paul wrote in 1 Timothy:

> Do not neglect your gift, which was given you through prophecy when the body of elders laid their hands on you. Be diligent in these matters; give yourself wholly to them so that everyone may see your progress. Watch your life and doctrine closely. Persevere in them because if you do, you will save both yourself and your hearers. (1 Timothy 4:14-16)

Peter would join Paul in writing about God holding believers accountable for the proper utilization of their gifts when he wrote in 1 Peter 4:10, "Each of you should use whatever gift you have received to serve others, as faithful stewards of God's grace in its various forms." (*New International Version Bible*, 1978/1993, 1 Peter 4:10) When God commands believers to be faithful stewards of God's grace, "He is telling us to faithfully and diligently administer our spiritual gifts that

He has entrusted to our care" (Hybels, 1990, p. 112). When we use our spiritual gifts, it is an act of worship. And as Paul reminds all believers, not merely vocational ministry leaders, in Romans 12, we are called to:

> Therefore, I urge you, brothers and sisters, in view of God's mercy, to offer your bodies as a living sacrifice, holy and pleasing to God—this is your true and proper worship. Do not conform to the pattern of this world, but be transformed by the renewing of your mind. Then you will be able to test and approve what God's will is—his good, pleasing, and perfect will. (Romans 12:1-2)

Paul would also remind us in Ephesians 4:1, "As a prisoner for the Lord, then, I urge you to live a life worthy of the calling you have received." (Ephesians 4:1)

> "AS A PRISONER FOR THE LORD, THEN, I URGE YOU TO LIVE A LIFE WORTHY OF THE CALLING YOU HAVE RECEIVED."
>
> **EPHESIANS 4:1**

CONCLUSION

As stated previously in chapter nine, perhaps no other topic is discussed more but understood less than spiritual gifts. Many believers do not have a proper Biblical understanding of spiritual gifts. As this chapter has revealed, perhaps this is because there are so many differing opinions on the origin, the continued presence or lack of spiritual gifts available to believers today, and how one may discover their gift if they believe that they still exist (by assessment, inventory, or experience), and how to use your gift once you have found it.

As this chapter points out, Jesus awarded believers these gifts at His ascension for our use after His Victory over Satan until he returns. I believe that these spiritual gifts are still available and useful to believers today and that we should "not be ignorant" as Paul challenges us (1 Corinthians 12:1). We should adhere to what Peter writes to us when he writes, "Each of you should use *whatever gift you have received* to serve others, as *faithful stewards of God's grace* in its various forms" (1 Peter 4:10). If we did not have spiritual gifts available to us we could not obey the four passages outlining these gifts in Romans 12:1-8, 1 Cor. 12:1-31, Ephesians 4:7-15, and 1 Peter 4:10-11.

CHAPTER ELEVEN
Important Factors for the
Proper Use of Your Spiritual Gift

Once you have prayerfully performed the necessary steps of discovering your spiritual gift by answering the questions in the previous chapter, completing the recommended inventories, or through serving locally, or going on an "experience" trip (Getz), to maximize your individual vocational calling, the following instruments, assessments, and profiles are very beneficial in helping you prayerfully consider your career options.

StrengthsFinder 2.0

A useful inventory available to help you better understand the spiritual gifting that God has entrusted to you is called StrengthsFinder 2.0. While this inventory is focused more on God-given leadership talents and abilities and would not necessarily be considered a "spiritual gifts" inventory, it certainly assists one in

> "DO YOU HAVE THE OPPORTUNITY TO DO WHAT YOU DO BEST EVERY DAY?"

understanding how God has uniquely wired a person with a specific set of gifts. The motivation of this assessment is to answer this question, "Do you have the opportunity to do what you do best every day?" Chances are that you don't. Often, one's natural (God-given, emphasis mine) talents go untapped. One devotes more time to addressing shortcomings from the cradle to the cubicle than developing strengths. Therefore, to help people uncover their gifts (gifts, emphasis mine), Gallup introduced the first version of its online assessment, StrengthsFinder, in 2001, which ignited a global conversation and helped millions to discover their top five talents. I highly recommend this assessment to you if you truly want to assess what you are genuinely gifted in doing with your life vocationally. Each book has a code and allows you to take an online assessment and determine your leadership qualities. Following is a summary chart of the four "domain" areas this inventory will provide you and the character qualities found in each domain.

4 DOMAINS OF LEADERSHIP STRENGTHS

EXECUTING	INFLUENCING	RELATIONSHIP BUILDING	STRATEGIC THINKING
Achiever	Activator	Adaptability	Analytical
Arranger	Command	Developer	Context
Belief	Communication	Connectedness	Futuristic
Consistency	Competition	Empathy	Ideation
Deliberative	Maximizer	Harmony	Input
Discipline	Self-Assurance	Includer	Intellection
Focus	Significance	Individualization	Learner
Responsibility	Woo	Positivity	Strategic
Restorative		Relator	

The Lead Like Jesus Model

Based on my research and life experience as a leader, another book that I would recommend for you as you seek God's vocational will for your life to assist you in the area of identifying and developing your spiritual gift is **Lead Like Jesus**. This book is particularly helpful if you are in a place of leadership or mentorship. While this book focuses on maximizing your God-ordained leadership capabilities, three of the models found in this book can also be very helpful in assisting you in discovering your vocational will.

The first model is the Transformational Leadership Model (see model below). As you can see, this model describes our leadership progression as we mature with education, preparation, and, most importantly, *experience*. According to this model, all leadership begins with **Personal Leadership**, you being able to exercise the self-discipline to lead yourself – physically, mentally, emotionally, intellectually, and spiritually. My good friends, Steve and Mary Lowe, have a wonderful book, <u>The Ecologies of Faith in a Digital Age,</u> that describes this process well if you are looking for assistance in this area of your life. Secondly, after you can lead yourself, you must develop the ability to teach another person in a **One-on-One Leadership** journey. This is best represented in the Biblical relationship of Paul instructing Timothy, the same way many of you lead and mentor others. I hope this book and my model become useful tools in your tool belt as you lead others.

Third is your ability to **Lead a Team.** As your leadership ability is growing and maturing, you now have the ability to lead a department, a small group, or a team well. Finally, as your leadership flourishes, you will mature to the top leadership level, **Organizational Leadership.** A leader who systematically grows and develops over time will eventually earn the right to lead businesses, organizations, corporations, ministries, and Boards.

I believe that these same four steps that apply to leadership and can be used in your journey of discovering God's vocational will for your life. You must discern your God-given passion individually (Personal Leadership). Next, you must determine your spiritual gifts, the purpose of this section, and confirm it with those spiritual mentors in your life (One-on-One Leadership). Third, you must "test" or "practice" your vocational interest by serving in this potential vocational area to confirm your calling (Team Leadership). And finally, once your passion, spiritual gift, and, as we will later discover, meet a need in others around you, you will be able to serve and lead in a vocational profession with passion and spiritual gifts entrusted to you (Organizational Leadership).

TRANSFORMATIONAL MODEL OF LEADERSHIP

1. PERSONAL LEADERSHIP
(OUTCOME = PERSPECTIVE)
Character, Trustworthiness

4. ORGANIZATIONAL LEADERSHIP
(OUTCOME = EFFECTIVENESS)

2. ONE-ON-ONE LEADERSHIP
(OUTCOME = TRUST)

3. TEAM LEADERSHIP
(OUTCOME = COMMUNITY)

Adapted from Lead Like Jesus (Blanchard and Hodges)

So, how do you develop these leadership abilities and transition from one leadership capability to the next? Great question. In <u>Lead Like Jesus</u>, the authors provide two helpful models that help you answer this question. I will summarize here, but I highly recommend adding this book to your library.

DEVELOPMENTAL MODEL OF LEADERSHIP

Adapted from *Lead Like Jesus* (Blanchard and Hodges)

The first model is called the Developmental Model of Leadership. This model describes leadership as progressing from developmental level one (**D1**) to level four (**D4**). A **D1** leader is an ***Enthusiastic Beginner*** with low competence but high commitment. A **D1** leader is very excited to be a new team member but has little experience in this new job, role, or organization (even if they have experience in a former organization).

A **D2** leader is a ***Disillusioned Learner*** with low to some competence but low commitment. This is the stage where many people seeking God's vocational will for their lives get "stuck." They want to believe that God has a plan for their lives, but they have been seeking it for so long with little to no success that they often feel that it does not exist. This is where 75% to 80% of the people I meet regularly find themselves. This is also why I have worked so hard to develop my model for you if you are one of these people searching for or leading others in making this decision.

A **D3** leader has fought their way past being disillusioned (**D2**), usually with the help of others, and has become a ***Capable but Cautious Performer*** who displays moderate to high competence but variable commitment. The **D3** developmental level experiences the highest level of growth. This motivated leader is rapidly acquiring new cognitive levels of understanding and matching physical capabilities and becoming a very effective, efficient, and skilled leader who needs little supervision and occasional reinforcement.

Over time this very skilled **D3** leader transforms into a **D4** leader, a ***Peak Performer*** with high competence and high commitment. This is the trained, qualified, experienced, effective, and highly capable leader - an expert in their field. A **D4** leader makes the right decisions, at the right times, for the right reasons that benefit both the individuals and the organizations they lead while leading, developing, and serving others. All effective organizations have a D4 leader.

Finally, once we understand *how* leaders are **developed** over time, the next logical question is *what* is necessary to help others develop from one sage to the next. The third model is a step-by-step sequence of helping us "mentor" others in their leadership development. These steps are useful as we systematically assist others in discovering God's vocational will.

The final model from <u>Lead like Jesus</u> that I feel is helpful is the "**S**" chart, which stands for "**Stage of Development**." You must know your people well enough to recognize what developmental level they are currently operating at and, more importantly, know what type of "coaching" they need to progress.

For example, the **D1** leader (Enthusiastic Beginner) needs **S1** "Directing." They need high directive and low supportive leadership. They need specific instruction, a template, a model, or a person to follow. They are not ready to make decisions independently or perform a skill alone.

The **D2** leader (Disillusioned Learner) needs **S2** "Coaching, " defined as high directive and supportive behavior. This is the most "critical" part of anyone's leadership development. The learner will quit if a proper coach is not involved with a **D2** disillusioned learner. They will leave school, a job, a team, a production, or even a marriage. In this state, a person is completely overwhelmed, sees no solution, and may even make sudden irrational decisions. In this book, I do not have the space to discuss all of the implications of people in this delicate stage, but any time people at any age and in any situation feel disillusioned and trapped, it is not healthy and often leads to anxiety, stress, strained relationships, and can even lead to permanent solutions to temporary problems. That is why coaches, mentors, or even professional counselors are critical in people's lives at this vital stage.

A **D3** person (Capable but Cautious Performer) needs **S3** "Supporting," which is low directive (they know "how" to perform a task) and highly supportive behavior. In other words, they now have the knowledge and skills but need more practice and experience. They occasionally ask questions but usually, seek confirmation that they are on the right track.

Finally, a **D4** (Peak Performer) only needs **S4** "Delegating." They require low directive and low supportive behavior. If you try to give a Peak Performer step-by-step instructions, it will insult them. It will also demonstrate that *you* do not know them or their capabilities well. When we have developed peak performers, we can tell them what needs to be done, and they can handle every aspect of completing that task, including the problem-solving required if changes need to be made. Our goal should be to develop Peak Performers in every area of the organizations that we lead. This motivates and inspires those we lead and frees us up to provide leadership for new programs, lead inexperienced staff in other areas, and design new adventures. Below is the Situational Leadership Chart II from Lead like Jesus, which combines the Developmental Level of those we lead with the types of Supportive Behavior (coaching) they need.

SITUATIONAL LEADERSHIP II MODEL

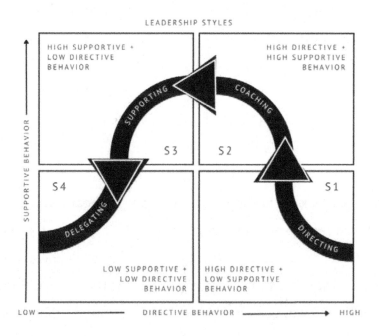

Adapted from *Lead Like Jesus* (Blanchard and Hodges)

PERSONALITY TYPES

While your God-given personality is not a spiritual gift, your temperament is God-ordained and important in utilizing your spiritual gifting. For example, your spiritual gift may be serving. But there are various ways to use this gift – both upfront and behind the scenes. You may find fulfillment and satisfaction by helping quietly in a task-oriented role like filling communion cups, preparing PowerPoint slides, assisting behind the scenes in functions like accounting, organizing (people or products), or taking inventories. On the other hand, you may possess the gift of service and love "people" and enjoy serving by parking cars, being a greeter, working at an information desk, answering phones, or giving tours.

This is not a book on personality types, but to properly assist you in discerning God's vocational will for your life, I would like to provide you with a brief overview of personality types. This information is important for you regardless of the vocation you discern using my model. If you need or desire a more comprehensive study on personality temperaments than provided here, I invite you to investigate the following personality profiles or other assessments in more detail independently.

THE DISC PERSONALITY PROFILE

In this simple but powerful personality profile, we recognize four basic temperaments God has given us. Dr. Robert Rohm is one of the most dynamic communicators of this D I S C profile. Attending Dr. Rohm's seminar live in 1995 revolutionized how I understood, related, communicated, and led people from that day forward. Dr. Rohm says that God designed you with a "motor." Your motor is either outgoing and fast-paced *or* reserved and slower-paced. Let's fill in the following chart if you are visual like me. Next to the blank at the top of the model labeled #1, write the word *Outgoing.* Now, at the bottom of the model, labeled #2, write the word *Reserved.*

In addition to your motor, Dr. Rohm also says people have a God-given "Compass" that directs them. People are either very *"task-oriented"* (high tech) or *"people-oriented"* (high touch). As both names imply, task-oriented people deeply desire to complete a task and celebrate when tasks are performed efficiently, effectively, correctly, and on time. These people have a low tolerance for incompetence, laziness, incomplete assignments, and mistakes.

On the other hand, people-oriented individuals deeply desire relationships and want to work in teams, with people, and for people. They may never complete or complete the task slowly, but they will know everyone's name and several personal facts about them (and probably their families). If you look at the model, on the left side, in blank #3, write the word *Task-oriented*. On the right side, in blank #4, write *People-oriented*.

Now, look at your chart. In the top left quadrant is Outgoing and Task-Oriented people. Dr. Rohm calls these people "D" personalities. Write the letter "D" in blank #5. Next to the "D" quadrant are people who are also Outgoing but are "People" oriented. Dr. Rohm describes these people as "I" personality types. Write the letter "I" in blank #6. Below the "I" are people who are Reserved and People-oriented. These are "S" personality types. Write the letter "S" in blank #7. And finally, next to the "S" quadrant are Reserved and Task-oriented people. These are "C" personality types. Write the letter "C" in blank #8.

FILL IN THE BLANKS

#1 _____

#5 _____   _____ #6

#3 _____   _____ #4

_____   _____

#8 _____   _____ #7

#2 _____

These are the four basic personality types. Understanding these personality types is important as you develop your spiritual gifts and lead others. Your spiritual gift will be enhanced, and your profession will be selected more accurately when you properly understand how God has "wired" you. For example, each personality type has a defined need, and when this need is not met, there becomes tension in any personal relationship.

For example, a "D" personality *needs challenge and control* because God has wired them to be dominant, driving, and determined. If you try to control someone (a co-worker, friend, your child) who is a "D" personality, they hear you say, "Do you want to fight?" Relationally, a better way to lead a "D" person is to say, "when you are ready, please do..... as long as it is done by tomorrow." Now they can "control" *when* they do it, *how* they do it, and even *IF* they are going to do it.

The "I" personality, *active* and *outgoing* but people-oriented, *needs recognition and approval*. It is all about relationships, socialization, and community for these people. They may not know the goal, mission, or *why* they are there, but they will one hundred percent understand *who* is there. They will also learn *many* personal facts about MOST of the people there. They care deeply about their friends. This can be both beautiful (when someone is lonely, needing a friend, or hurting) and disastrous (when an important task needs to be accomplished – especially if it is in a time-sensitive manner).

The "S" personality is *reserved* and *people-oriented*. These people want everyone to get along because they are sensitive and sympathetic. These non-confrontational peacekeepers deeply desire peace, harmony, and unity in any family, social setting, organization, or church. These people will stay silent when upset, reserved when there is chaos, and serve quietly when others either will not or do not. The "S" personality needs *appreciation and security*. Your willingness, ability, and capability to be confrontational (given by God) deeply impact the vocation that God has for you.

Finally is the "C" personality. These people are *reserved* and *task-oriented*. These people have LOTS of questions. They do not ask questions to irritate you. They just genuinely have a ton of questions racing in their mind. And surprisingly, they *don't even ask* many of the questions that are swirling at a dizzying pace in their brains all the time. They are problem solvers. They are cautious (measure, measure, measure, "cut"). A "D" will say, "measure once, cut it now, close enough, and get the job finished." An "I" will say, "who's here? How long can we stay? Who brought the snacks? Oh, someone is cutting something?" The "S" really hopes you don't ask them to cut. They do not want to make a mistake. The "S" is sure the "D" will do it faster, the "C" will do it more accurately, the "I" will have more fun, and they would assume someone else cut. But, if you need them to do it, they are willing, but they are not the best choice. The "C" needs *quality answers and value*. And they will keep asking questions until they are satisfied.

ANOTHER PERSONALITY PROFILE PERSPECTIVE

Another personality profile perspective is offered by the ancient Greek physician, surgeon, and philosopher Galen (c. AD 129–200), described in his dissertation *De temperamentis* - the first typology of temperaments. This typology was based on the four bodily fluids called "humors," namely black bile, yellow bile, phlegm, and blood, that directly affect an individual's personality, behavior, and health and considers the balance and imbalance of temperament pairs. Hippocrates and Galen were among the first scientists to suggest that these fluids affect one's temperament. According to Galen, the balance of these "humors" result in one of these four temperament categories (or personality types): *sanguine* (being optimistic and social), an "I," *choleric* (being short-tempered and irritable), the "D," *melancholic* (being analytical and quiet) the "C," and *phlegmatic* (being relaxed and peaceful), the "S."

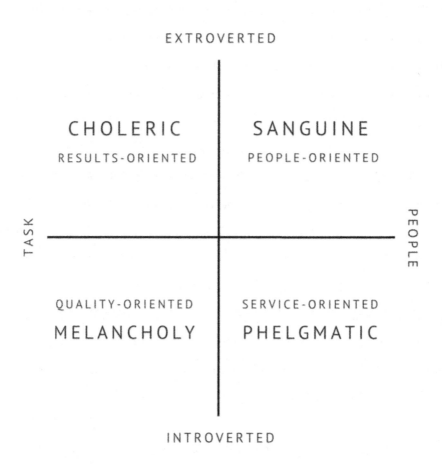

EXTROVERTED

CHOLERIC
RESULTS-ORIENTED

SANGUINE
PEOPLE-ORIENTED

TASK

PEOPLE

QUALITY-ORIENTED
MELANCHOLY

SERVICE-ORIENTED
PHELGMATIC

INTROVERTED

THE FOUR ANIMALS PERSONALITY PROFILE

Another popular author and speaker, Dr. Trent, developed another way to assess one's personality that is much simpler and quicker than some more complex instruments. Dr. Trent writes, "during my doctoral program, I studied many tests created to help people see their strengths. However, I quickly discovered that while most were very helpful, almost all of them were extremely complicated to take, and even the results were hard to understand. For example, one popular personality assessment instrument uses 364 questions to assess a person's strengths and weaknesses. You must also be certified to explain what the answers to those questions mean!"

So, based on his experience and research, Dr. Trent created a tool that was accurate and much easier to understand and that someone could take and read the results in three to five minutes. The assessment aimed to show people their unique, God-given strengths. Dr. Trent's simplified personality profile uses animals to describe the four common personality types used in many well-known models. These animals are the Lion (D in the D I S C, the Choleric), the Otter (I in the D I S C, the Sanguine), the Retriever (S – in the D I S C model, the Phlegmatic), and a Beaver (C in the D I S C, the Melancholic).

LION   OTTER   RETRIEVER   BEAVER

Understanding personality types that God has supernaturally endowed and ordained is *not* meant to "*label people*" but to help us better "understand" people. We are all created differently. The sooner we recognize these differences, the better we can relate to our family, siblings, spouses, friends, and co-workers. Your long-term vocational satisfaction will be a combination of your spiritual gifting (which makes tasks easy for you) and your personality temperament (which helps you understand yourself and lead others well based on your personality). We will associate with different "spheres" of influence and interact with various social networks daily. The better we understand our personality and recognize the *needs of others*, the better we can work with and lead them. We will discuss "*needs*" in future chapters.

OUTGOING

dominant driving
determined

inspiring interesting
interactive

D

CHOLERIC
L I O N

I

SANGUINE
O T T E R

TASK-
ORIENTED

PEOPLE-
ORIENTED

cautious competent
controlled

supportive stable
sympathetic

C

MELANCHOLY
B E A V E R

S

PHELGMATIC
R E T R I E V E R

RESERVED

The following page contains a chart of two scenarios that may help you better understand how different personality temperaments respond to different situations.

SCENARIOS

#1 YOU ARE RAKING LEAVES

D (LION)
Go get a leaf blower. I am definitely going to hire someone else to do this.

I (OTTER)
Who's coming? How long can we stay? Will there be snacks? I can bring coffee. Does anyone need a ride there? I can take anyone home!

S (RETRIEVER)
I will do anything you need. I will bring rakes, trash bags, and gloves if needed. But I don't have to if someone else would rather. I might not get the best gloves or the right size trash bags.

C (BEAVER)
We have six rakes. We will work in pairs of two. Each team will rake a six-foot straight line, then pick up the leaves on their row. We will be done in an hour. Why are we starting so late? Why do we only have six people? Why don't we have more bags to pick these up?

#2 A TEACHER ASKS A CLASS, "WHO DISCOVERED AMERICA?"

D (LION)
Blurts out immediately, "COLUMBUS" very loudly with authority.

I (OTTER)
"OH, UM, UM, Pick Me, Pick Me!" while Jumping up and down out of their seat, and maybe even on their desk!

S (RETRIEVER)
Please don't call on me.

C (BEAVER)
"What exactly do you mean by discover? I am sure you want me to say Christopher Columbus, and I will, but the Native Americans were actually already here."

SAMPLE VOCATION CHART

10 EXAMPLES OF EACH PERSONALITY TYPE

D (LION)	I (OTTER)	S (RETRIEVER)	C (BEAVER)
choleric	sanguine	phlegmatic	melancholy
Administrators	Actors	Admin Assistants	Accountants
Athletes	Broadcasters	Childcare Workers	Airline Pilots
Coaches	Comedians	Counselors	Bankers/Bookkeepers
Directors	Entertainers	Diplomats	Computer Programmers
Entrepreneurs	Evangelists	Flight Attendants	Engineers
Executives	Event Coordinators	HR Directors	Lawyers
Lawyers	Flight Attendants	Managers	Military Intelligence
Military Officers	PR Directors	Nurses	Physicians/Pharmacists
Police Officers	Salespersons	Secretaries	Scientist/Researchers
Supervisors	Travel Agents	Teachers	Statisticians

CONCLUSION

So, the second practical step in discerning God's individual vocational will for your life is for you to prayerfully discover God's ordained spiritual gifting by completing any of several of the spiritual gift inventories discussed in this chapter, or as Gextz recommended, to volunteer in several areas that you feel led to serve or take a mission trip (domestic or international) and see what God does.

Getz's method is how God touched my good friend and founder of a big camp in Georgia. As a successful banker, he took a mission trip to Ukraine, and God changed the trajectory of his life. Because of his faithfulness and obedience, hundreds of campers and staff have been changed forever as he and his team lead *unforgettable* camping experiences at this camp every day. As we have just learned, if we do not know and are not using our spiritual gift(s), we are not walking faithfully in obedience to God's individual vocational will for our lives.

Next, once you have figured out your spiritual gift, investigate your God-ordained leadership abilities and your personality temperament. Knowing your leadership style and personality strengths, weaknesses, and basic needs will help you discern how to direct your passion, use your spiritual

> IF WE DO NOT KNOW AND ARE NOT USING OUR SPIRITUAL GIFT(S), WE ARE NOT WALKING FAITHFULLY IN OBEDIENCE TO GOD'S INDIVIDUAL VOCATIONAL WILL FOR OUR LIVES.

gifts more effectively, and live at peace with yourself and others.

We spend a lot of discretionary time on trivial things today like sports, video games, shopping, surfing the internet, and binging Netflix, Hulu, or Disney Plus. I would *challenge* you if you are a **D,** *invite* you if you are an **I** (and do it with a friend), allow you the *freedom* to do it on your own *at your own pace* if you are an **S,** and *critically consider* if you are a **C,** discovering your spiritual gift, your personality type, and professions where your spiritual gifts are vital to the success of that organization. In other words, they need you!

Add *step two* to the model below by writing **"Spritual Gift"** in the shaded oval. We will address the third and final critical element of *need* in the following section.

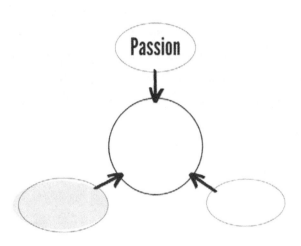

DISCERNING GOD'S INDIVIDUAL VOCATIONAL WILL
THE OGLESBY MODEL

SECTION FOUR

NEED

Finally, the third element in this practical three-step model for discerning God's vocational will for your life is a proper understanding of *need*. The following sections will explain how God designed all humans with *internal and external needs* and how internally God-ordained needs drive us to meet the personal, local, regional, national, and even global external *needs* of others in our world.

CHAPTER TWELVE

NEED: What Area of Need is God Calling YOU to Meet?

The third step for discerning God's individual vocational will for one's life is to evaluate where on the planet God has a **need** for someone with your passion and spiritual gift to serve. When it comes to assessing needs, there are **two** primary factors. First is your *internal* need to feel *loved* and to *belong*. This need is met best in our relationship with God, made available to us in the birth, life, death, burial, and resurrection of His One and only Son, Jesus. Until we meet our deepest need for a relationship with Jesus, we will search a wide range of other avenues to fill this internal need. When we accept this free gift of salvation, we "belong" to the family of God and become co-heirs with Christ (Romans 8:17).

> ALL PEOPLE HAVE AN INTERNAL DESIRE TO BE LOVED, NOTICED, BELONG, AND MAKE A VALUABLE CONTRIBUTION TO THEIR VOCATIONAL PURSUITS.

We also have an inner need to feel valuable to a family, an operation, an organization, a ministry, or a cause. In short, all people have an internal desire to be loved, noticed, belong, and make a valuable contribution to their vocational pursuits. Abraham Maslow, and Maslow's Hierarchy of Needs, is the most noteworthy example of outlining the process of helping one realize their peak performance of vocational self-actualization by assisting humans in understanding *how their needs must be met internally before one can successfully meet the needs of others.* As pictured on the following page, Maslow (1943) outlined that for you to feel valued and needed, your physiological needs, safety needs, love and belonging needs, and self-esteem needs must be met and satisfied to reach the ultimate goal of your performance – self-actualization - reaching your full inner potential (McLeod, 2018).

Second is one's desire to serve and make a difference by meeting an *external* global need in our world. God has created people to meet the needs of others in our world. This list of potential needs is vast, and God gives people opportunities to love, heal, provide for, rescue, and deliver people from various challenges based on human needs. Jesus, of course, was the best leader that the planet has ever seen at meeting people's physical and spiritual needs.

How does one find a job to serve a cause or a people group that one is passionate about and has the spiritual gift to help? According to Mattson and Miller Jr. (1999), in their book, *Finding a Job You Can Love*, an estimated 50-80% of working Americans are in the wrong line of work. Therefore, Mattson and Miller Jr. offer to lead their readers through a personal inventory of discovering who they are and what they were meant to do.

By viewing work as a sacred calling, Mattson and Miller (1999) show how to assess one's unique God-given design, identify one's specific gifts, harness one's genuine interests and motivations, avoid confusion and self-deception and discover one's individual vocational calling that brings true delight. Mattson and Miller (1999) explain that being in a job or role suitable for our gifts is essential in fulfilling God's will. Whether one is looking for a *first-time vocation or a new career change*, they offer both clear thinking and practical direction on glorifying God by enjoying the work He has created one to do. Mattson and Miller (1999) conclude that all people desire to make a meaningful contribution to their vocational employment team and work harder when they feel valued and necessary to the overall task being performed.

Miller (2012) writes that all men and women were made to live in the reality that God has made, the reality of the kingdom of God. Within this reality is vision, a compelling vision. Vision is one of the most basic of all human needs. This is affirmed in scripture: "Where there is no vision, the people perish." (Proverbs 29:18). All of our lives are driven by a vision. But not all visions are accurate, nor are they equally fulfilling. A God-ordained vision fulfills a need. This could be meeting a physical, mental, emotional, or spiritual need in the lives of others. This could also be completing a personal, corporate, organizational, or ministry need in the workplace (Lu and Gursoy, 2016). God designed humans to meet a need and to feel needed. If one is not doing either of these items, one is less fulfilled than God has designed (Schreiner, 2018).

As the church enters the twenty-first century, it is largely divided into two groups, each with a very different understanding of the kingdom of God. The first understands the kingdom of God as mystical, invisible, heavenly, and in the future. These Christians state that Jesus is Lord of all, but His kingdom will affect things here on earth only when Christ returns at the end of history. This school of thought struggles to help people discover their importance in meeting an earthly need (Nash & McLennan, 2001).

VISION IS ONE OF THE MOST BASIC OF ALL HUMAN NEEDS.

The second group, in contrast, understands that the kingdom of God is to make a difference - here and now. Too often, however, these people focus on social and political concerns and use human means to establish God's kingdom to exclude evangelism and future aspects of the Kingdom. Each of these views is incomplete (Miller, 2012).

So, how do you discover God's most critical areas of need? Most simply stated, Miller (2012) says the kingdom of God exists wherever God reigns. That God has no limit in time, location, or realm. Almighty God, who always was, is, and shall be, is the king of the heavens and the earth. He is the Lord of history as well as eternity. He is living and present in both the spiritual and material realms (Miller, 2012).

As the so-called developed world enters the twenty-first century, too often, westerners find that the secular worldview has reduced work to a career and life to an endless consumption of things. As a result, many live without hope and purpose, and for many, work and life itself carry little, if any, meaning. High suicide rates, addictions to alcohol, drugs, pornography and sex, divorce, and increased loneliness, even in crowded apartment complexes, are all signs of the death of the soul of man (Wright, 2007).

People's lives and work are diminished from what God would have them be. The marketplace determines many people's value or worth and the money they make. Today, to maintain this lifestyle, many people sacrifice what matters the most - family, friends, marriages, and Christian fellowship - to pursue success, prestige, fame, and power to meet the other goals prized by the world. All too often, there is a direct relationship between our escalating material prosperity and our increasing moral and spiritual poverty (Shaw & Gupa, 2004).

According to Bugbee (2005), for both westerners and peoples of the developing world, life and work have been separated from the daily, practical values and intentions of the kingdom of God in the world - those things that give our work real value and meaning. This separation marks the lives of believers as well. *Too many Christians separate work and worship.* Life is in two different compartments. The first is the religious and spiritual life that takes place in church and on Sunday. Christians are primarily proactive and consciously engaging in Christian activities in this compartment. The second is work, and their lives in this community exist from Monday through Saturday. And in this part of life, Christians are, at best, reactive. There is no connection between these two parts of life. For too many Christians, the Bible speaks to the spiritual aspect of life, but it is the values of our national culture that govern most of life. As a result, individuals and entire nations are not reaching their God-given potential, leaving many unmet needs in our society.

The solution for this fragmentation is the common foundation for the reconnection of our lives and our work to God's mission and His Kingdom - becoming truly Christ's body with the Risen Christ as its head (Bugbee, 2005). The kingdom for which we work will not only come with all of its Glory when Christ returns, but it is the kingdom that also is currently at hand and is coming today in tangible ways through each Christian's life as they pursue fulfilling god-ordained vocations (Miller, 2012).

Miller (2012) writes that we need to help Christians *reconnect* their lives with their work in advancing God's kingdom and help people meet the spiritual needs in our world. A key to achieving this is developing a Biblical worldview and powerful vision that enables one to understand that their work is a term of calling and vocation. Thus their lives are more consistently glorifying God regardless of their chosen field of endeavor (Nash & McLennan, 2001). This process transforms one's life and work into a call from God Himself, and the relationship that one has to their work and God becomes meshed together, no longer two separate entities (Miller, 2012). *That is the purpose for this new three-step model!*

CONCLUSION

In this chapter, we discovered that we all have a God-ordained *internal need to be loved, belong, and to be valued* and *an external need to be a part of the solution to a global problem*, either domestically or internationally. Abraham Maslow, and Maslow's Hierarchy of Needs, is the most noteworthy example of outlining the process of helping one realize their peak performance of vocational self-actualization by assisting humans in understanding ***how their needs must be met internally before one can successfully meet the needs of others.***

So, how do you find a job to serve a cause or a people group that you are passionate about and have the spiritual gift to help? According to Mattson and Miller Jr. (1999), in their book, *Finding a Job You Can Love*, an estimated 50-80 percent of working Americans are in the wrong line of work. Therefore, Mattson and Miller Jr. offer to lead their readers through a personal inventory of discovering who they are and what they were meant to do.

Many people's lives and work are diminished from what God would have them be. Many people's value or worth is determined by the marketplace and the money they make. Today, to maintain this lifestyle, many people sacrifice what matters the most - family, friends, marriages, and Christian fellowship - to pursue success, prestige, fame, and power to meet the other goals prized by the world. All too often, there is a direct relationship between our escalating *material prosperity* and our increasing moral and *spiritual poverty* (Shaw & Gupa, 2004).

CHAPTER THIRTEEN
Meeting External Needs

job crafting:
meeting the needs of
employees and clients

Another vital form of assessing *external* needs in the marketplace is a performance theory called job crafting. Job crafting describes how employees redesign their jobs and ways to foster job satisfaction and engagement, resilience, and thriving internally at work (Wrzesniewski & Dutton, 2001). Your job is a collection of tasks and interpersonal relationships assigned to one person in an organization (Ilgen & Hollenbeck, 1992). Job crafting theory elaborates on classic job design theory that focuses on the top-down process of managers designing jobs for their employees (Hackman & Oldham, 1976). Employees in any formally designated job are often motivated to customize their careers to fit their motives, strengths, and passions. Job crafting describes how employees utilize opportunities to customize their jobs by actively changing their tasks and interactions with others. Crafting assignments to use a team member's *gifts* also places employees in an area of their *passion*, which helps employees meet both personal and professional *needs* – the reason for job crafting. Those who perform these revisions are called job crafters. Research suggests they can employ at least three different forms of job crafting to help employers design job descriptions that enable employees to utilize their internal passions and giftings better to serve the *external* needs of the ministry, business, or organization.

First, job crafters can expand or limit the boundaries of their jobs by taking on fewer or more tasks, expanding or diminishing the scope of functions, or changing how they perform tasks. Second, job crafters can transform their relationships at work by altering the nature or extent of their interactions with other people. Third, job crafters can cognitively change their jobs by altering how they perceive tasks (Berg et al., 2008).

Meeting Global Needs

One of the critical elements in assessing God's ordained individual vocational will for your life is using your passion and spiritual gift to meet a global need. While the limited space in this book does not allow me to adequately provide a comprehensive list of all of the global needs that exist today (i.e., teachers for inner cities, organizations fighting sex trafficking, providing clean drinking water to third world countries, Christian mission organizations, disaster relief organizations, assisting senior citizens, addressing the growing mental and emotional issues in our culture today, etc.) this section will give you a template to follow to investigate the global need that is God has placed on your heart and is most pressing to you.

RESOURCE
LINKS

DEMOGRAPHIC NEEDS
(i.e., impoverished families, single-parent households, foster children, clean drinking water, etc.)

- https://usa.gov/statistics
- https://census.gov/data.html

HUMANITARIAN NEEDS
(i.e., emergency response to natural disaster organizations, clean drinking water in third world countries, world hunger)

- https://samaritanspurse.org
- https://www.compassion.com

FAITH AND CULTURE NEEDS
(i.e., organizations that lobby for faith-based solutions to poverty, equity in schools, and legal issues)

- https://barna.com
- https://wallbuilders.com
- https://frc.org

EVANGELISM NEEDS
(i.e., Christian mission-sending organizations and churches)

- https://www.imb.org
- https://gonowmissions.com/

If that is the case, you may use this same research method to discover how you may become involved in addressing the global need that you are passionate about and have giftings to utilize in serving an existing organization and becoming a part of the solution, or perhaps even becoming the founder of an organization to address one of these areas of need that you are passionate about solving. On the previous page, the resource links provide examples of global needs and resources available to investigate how to become involved and understand the career options that can help you become involved in the solution.

CONCLUSION

In the diagram below, write the word "Need" in the shaded oval. You now have all three elements required to facilitate discerning God's vocational will for your life. But the most important step is next! How are these three elements related?

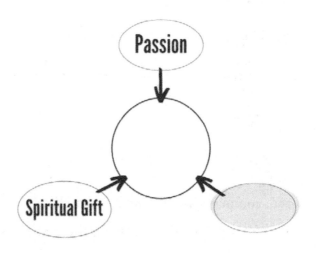

DISCERNING GOD'S INDIVIDUAL VOCATIONAL WILL
THE OGLESBY MODEL

SECTION FIVE

PUTTING IT ALL TOGETHER: THE INTERSECTION POINT OF PASSION, SPIRITUAL GIFT, AND NEED

As previously stated, there is very little research regarding how people discern God's individual vocational will for their lives. Hopefully, after reviewing the theoretical framework above, one can now see how each of these three practical steps of discovering one's passion, spiritual gift, and desire to meet an internal need and a need in the life of another person, people group, or organization can lead you to prayerfully discovering the vocational calling that God has placed inside of you.

CHAPTER FOURTEEN
Discerning God's Individual
Vocational Will: The Oglesby Model

As the diagram illustrates, all three critical elements (passion, spiritual gift, and need) are essential for discovering God's vocational will for your life. Based on the theological and theoretical studies cited in the previous chapters, I believe that where these three God-ordained elements intersect is the zone God has specifically ordained you to pursue (Psalm 139:13-16, Ephesians 2:10) for your life. Vygotsky (1978) refers to this type of intersection point as the Zone of Proximal Development (ZPD). He defines this zone as "the distance between the actual development level determined by independent problem solving and the level of potential development as determined through problem-solving under adult guidance, or in collaboration with more capable peers" (p. 86).

As mentioned earlier in this book, this "zone" of your individual vocational will is much different than the "dot" proposed by Friesen.

My model does not attempt to send you looking for the proverbial "needle in the haystack" or the elusive "dot" of one specific and right answer, but rather to give you a reflective tool to apply the "way of wisdom" that Friesen proposes by making decisions based on "evaluating data, devoting sufficient time to the process of decision making, seeking mature counsel, rightly applying scripture, and utilization of sound reasons (Friesen, p. 252).

That is what my model desires for you as you investigate your God-given passion, spiritual gifts, and needs. As the diagram below illustrates, my model fits perfectly into Friesen's proposed "way of wisdom" but also gives you a "model" to use within this area of "freedom" to help you discern God's vocational will for your life.

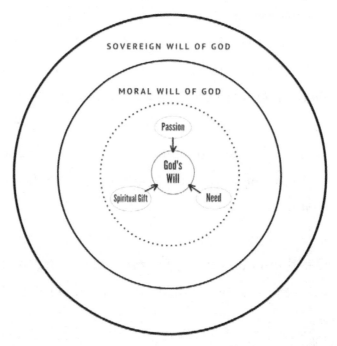

Vygotsky (1978) believed that when a student is in the *zone of proximal development* for a particular task (like discerning God's vocational will), providing appropriate assistance *will give the student enough boost to achieve the mission.* To assist a person in moving through the zone of proximal development, educators and mentors (I would add ministry leaders) are encouraged to focus on *three essential components* which aid the learning process:

The presence of someone with knowledge and skills beyond that of the learner (a more knowledgeable other, *in our case, a mentor* (parent, coach, youth pastor, etc.).

Social interactions with a skillful tutor allow learners to observe and practice their skills. For example, someone to *assist a learner in completing each assessment provided to help them discover their passion, spiritual gift, and a need* they feel emotionally drawn.

Scaffolding, or supportive activities provided by the educator, or a more competent peer, to support the student as they are led through the ZPD. *These have been provided for you throughout this book.*

Christian leaders can use these three steps to assist students in the self-evaluation and introspection process to help them discover God's passion, spiritual gift, and need that God has placed inside every believer. **The center intersection point (the zone) of these three essential** *criteria is God's individual vocational will for your life.* When you discover this *"zone"* for discerning your vocational calling accurately, several incredible things will happen for you:

If passion, spiritual gift, and need are three legs of a camera tripod, the intersection *"zone"* connecting these critical elements where the camera would sit up top is the *zone for God's individual vocational will for your life.*

1) In this zone, you will be *passionate about serving* because God has placed inside of you a passion for a cause, people group, organization, or solution to a global problem.

> THE CENTER INTERSECTION POINT (THE ZONE) OF THESE THREE ESSENTIAL CRITERIA IS GOD'S INDIVIDUAL VOCATIONAL WILL FOR YOUR LIFE.

2) In this zone, you will *utilize your spiritual gift to intentionally further the Kingdom.* Your work will intrinsically motivate you because it comes from God and will be easy to execute because it is in your God-ordained supernatural gifting.

3) In this zone, you will meet an *internal need* to belong and be valued and an *external global need* by being a part of the

solution to meet the needs of others physically, mentally, emotionally, and spiritually both domestically and worldwide.

When you discover this zone, you will be *passionate*, energetic, intentional, *spiritually gifted*, and meeting a spiritual or a physical *need* in the lives of others, thus *fulfilling God's will for your life*. God will be glorified (the Chief End of Humanity) by your faithful and obedient service to Him, regardless of profession. You will then live a life of obedience, and the Kingdom will expand (Matthew 28:16-20).

When you discover this zone, you will *experience fewer mental health issues* like anxiety, stress, panic attacks, and even physical illnesses due to the inability to cope healthily with the stressors and challenges of working in an environment that is not life-giving.

When you discover this zone, *you will experience the peace of God* that surpasses all understanding because you will be walking in obedience to your God-ordained calling.

When you discover this zone, *you will experience the stability our relationship with God* is meant to provide through His Holy Spirit during life's storms. Like the Apostle Paul, storms will still hit (2 Corinthians 11:21-28), but when you know that you are *walking in*

God's purpose for your life, you will have a grounded anchor point during these trials and storms.

The diagram below illustrates the intersection zone of these three critical elements. This *zone* of God's individual vocational will occurs when all three aspects for discerning God's personal vocational will for your life are carefully and prayerfully discovered, and the intersection point of these three vital elements is implemented into your life.

For example, if you have completed the model and determined that you are supposed to be a youth pastor, this "*zone*" will not necessarily tell you to go be the youth pastor of a *specific* church, but it will help you determine that you are called to be a youth pastor and allow you to access based on your *passion* (love to work with youth, problem solve, mentor), *your spiritual gifts* (teaching, administration, serving), type of *personality* (are you a D I S, or C), and what kind of youth ministry *need* God has called you to fulfill (small rural church community, medium-sized church, large muli-site church), para-church (FCA, YoungLife, Cru), camp, or urban inner-city? So within your "*zone*," you still have plenty of options to serve faithfully as God leads and directs you by His Holy Spirit. I believe the late Garry Friesen would appreciate you being able to use his "way of wisdom' and not experience the exhaustion and frustration of looking for the "dot."

This same type of freedom within the *"zone"* exists if you are called to be a *teacher* (what age, what location, what subject based on passion, spiritual gift, and need), be a *doctor* (based on passion, gifting, and need), be an *attorney* (based on passion, gifting, and need), or *any other field.* The *"zone"* of God's vocational will allows you to be *faithful* while also having the *freedom to serve God in various areas, positions, and locations* within your vocational discipline that you have discovered.

In this *"zone,"* you can also maneuver within each area (passion, spiritual gift, and need) of your calling as your experience, knowledge, and skills improve over time. Or, once you discover your

THE GOAL OF THIS MODEL IS NOT TO NARROW YOUR KINGDOM USEFULNESS OR VOCATIONAL OPTIONS BUT RATHER TO HELP YOU LIVE A FAITHFUL AND OBEDIENT LIFE WITH THE FREEDOM TO MOVE AS THE LORD LEADS YOU.

vocational will, you can *transfer previously learned skills* from a previous vocation to this newly discovered area of God's vocational will. You can serve areas of your passion based on your gifts and meet needs in various areas – domestically and internationally. The goal of this model is *NOT* to narrow your Kingdom usefulness or vocational options but rather to help you live a faithful and obedient life with the freedom to move as the Lord leads you.

CONCLUSION

Below is the completed Oglesby Model for Discerning God's Individual Vocational Will for your life, illustrating all three components and the "*zone*" of God's will for your life. As mentioned, I have used this model for many years to assist hundreds, if not thousands, of students discover God's vocational will for their lives with remarkable success.

In the final chapter, I will share with you that I am not only the originator of this model, but also the *result* of it. I will share my personal journey with you. I have also included a very short summary of my dissertation findings in the Appendix if you are interested. I am proud of you for finishing my book, and I will be praying for you on your continued journey to discover God's good, pleasing, and perfect will for your life! Stay in the raft, and listen to your guide!

DISCERNING GOD'S INDIVIDUAL VOCATIONAL WILL
THE OGLESBY MODEL

CHAPTER FIFTEEN

My Story, the Originator, and an Example of the Model

Not only did I (with God's inspiration and direction) develop the model outlined in this book based on my research as a tool to help others, but I am also a product of this model. After sitting across from high school and college students at Carolina Creek Christian Camps for 15 years, and now working with college students every day at Liberty University, I knew antidotally that this model has helped many students discover God's vocational will for their lives.

Then, after completing my dissertation study, which showed astounding statistical results, including that 95% percent of the 1,000 college students had been asked, "what do you want to do when you grow up?" over 94% understood and could use this model two-weeks after the presentation, 85% reported that this model had a significant impact on how they view their vocational futures, and over 20% changed their major, what I knew antidotally was confirmed.

Therefore, I desired to develop a more streamlined version of my dissertation study to present the results based on my research and my simple three-step model to help as many people as possible answer one of life's most asked and perplexing questions, "What am I supposed to do with my life, and how do I figure it out?"

Honestly, I never imagined writing a book, but I was challenged by a mentor and author who told me that people who have valuable information that God has divinely imparted through both research and experience and do not write books are **selfish**. People who know me well know that I deeply desire to meet and serve the needs of others (one of my spiritual gifts is serving, and I am an "S" personality type).

Even the thought, or the accusation, of being perceived as **selfish** has bothered me for several years. This friend, and author, meant that many people die and take their research, life experience, and wisdom to the grave. However, if they had merely written a book or shared this information with others, more people could have benefitted from the lessons they learned and the wisdom they gained.

Therefore, after many years of teaching this model and completing a dissertation study to scientifically validate this model's overwhelming effectiveness, I agreed to write the book you are holding. I hope that this book will help many people on their spiritual journey discern God's vocational will for their lives, live at peace, and share the truth of the gospel with others as a result of finding their place in the center of God's will based on their God-ordained *passion*, *spiritual gift(s),* and discovering the area of *need* that is of utmost importance to them. I am also a product of this three-step practical model. I combined my passion and my spiritual gifts and discovered a need where I could be at the center of God's vocational will for my life. Here, briefly, is my story.

PASSION

I was blessed to be raised in a Christian home with Bible-believing, teaching, and serving parents. My father was also a bi-vocational camp director. Before I could walk, I started attending Christian camps and have walked in camping ministry my entire life. In fact, my first summer not at summer camp followed my first year teaching at Liberty University. Therefore, it should not surprise anyone that I am passionate about camp. I tell my students that I am a camp-a-holic, a camp "junkie." I love everything about camp!

I love the laughter and energy of recreation during field games, under a pavilion, or in a pool. I love leading, watching, and listening to kids creating memories together behind ski boats on tubes and banana boats, flying through the air on zip lines, and climbing rock walls and vertical playpens. I love witnessing campers circled under shady areas alone with a Bible in their lap or a small group having meaningful discussions with their peers and college-aged counselors. I love an auditorium, worship center, gymnasium, or outdoor amphitheater filled with elementary, middle school, or high school campers with their hands raised, fully immersed, freely, and uninhibitedly worshiping God with their peers (especially led by my long-term worship leader and best friend, Denbigh Cherry).

The love, the receptiveness to God's Word, and the deep desire to apply God's Word to their lives not only at camp but to take it home with them, share it with their friends, and use it as a roadmap for life has driven me to serve this arena my entire life. In short, camp is a safe place to *experience* God and make life-long commitments like very few places or experiences anywhere else. And I have committed my entire personal and professional life to serve the Christian camping profession because it is my *passion*.

This *passion* was necessary for me (and my wife) to persevere for nine years when attempting to share this passion and vision for a new non-denominational camp with others in the Houston, Texas, area. I had completed extensive research and been told by Christian Camping International (CCI), later re-named Christian Camp and Conference Association (CCCA), that Houston, Texas, was the largest metropolitan area in the United States that was underserved in the area of Christian camping. So, based on this *need,* my wife and I, having been married just one month, moved to Houston, Texas, and began to share this *passion and vision* with others. And *passion* would be required. There were many sleepless and tear-filled nights over *nine years* when we often asked God *to fulfill this vision or remove this dream and passion* from us. It took nine years for us to meet the first donor couple willing to believe in and financially support this passionate vision.

SPIRITUAL GIFT

Before moving to Houston, Texas, I knew, based on some of these same inventories, assessments, and life experiences presented in this book, that I had the spiritual gifts of teaching, serving, and administration. My StrengthsFinder 2.0 five leadership qualities are belief, relator, achiever, developer, and responsibility. At rest, I am an "**S**" personality (a pastor, shepherd, and teacher), but professionally I have operated in a "**D**" role (visionary, take charge, administrator, leader) for most of my career, which is also very comfortable for me now, but it took several years to develop.

During these nine years of trying to build this camp in Houston, the Lord allowed me to use my athletic training degrees and national certification to serve as the Director of Sports Medicine at a medium size private Christian university and teach college courses in the Kinesiology department. In addition, I was also traveling and preaching regularly to teenagers at camps and retreats. I was also privileged to assist a professional NBA basketball team who shared our facilities as a practice site and serve a term as a volunteer athletic trainer at the USA Olympic Training Center in Chula Vista, California.

After several years, using my gifts of teaching and administration at this college and in these roles, I served as an Assistant Administrator and as the Administrator for a private Christian school in the Houston area. Again, my spiritual gifts of teaching, leading a team, serving, and administration were utilized daily, but I was **not passionate** about these roles in Christian education.

GOD LOVES US TOO MUCH TO ALLOW US TO WALK IN PROLONGED DISOBEDIENCE OR FORGET WHAT HE HAS CALLED US TO DO FOR HIM WHILE WE ARE HERE ON EARTH.

So, while very blessed to serve in these roles and minister to these families, I did not possess the "*fire*" internally that I possessed for Christian camp ministry. I could have easily compromised and decided not to pursue my **passion**, settled or gotten "trapped" in this school setting, and forgotten my true passion (like many adults described in the previous chapters). But my **passion** was **camp**. I know this because, even though I was serving others and making a difference, I was constantly thinking about camp – building a camp, preaching at camp, the activities at camp, and the evangelism and discipleship that occur at camp. Also, I know that it was from God because it would not leave. I could not get rid of it. God loves us too much to allow us to walk in prolonged disobedience or forget what He has called us to do for Him while we are here on earth. And I deeply desired to use His gifts to build a brand new non-denominational Christian sports camp for the city of Houston, no matter what it would take or how long it would take.

This passion for using my spiritual gifts drove me to work tirelessly for nine years to share my vision, write a business plan, and pray for the Lord's will to be done for the greater Houston and southwest Texas area. After nine years, I met our founding board chairman, and soon after, his wife and the gifts of teaching and administration were about to finally be utilized for my desired *passion*. I love the story of the tightrope walker who is going to walk above Nigeria Falls. Before walking out, he asked the crowd, "Who believes I can make it all the way across?" The crowd roared with applause. Then he said, "if anyone *really* believes, let them climb on my back." After nine years, our board chairman was willing to climb on my back, and I (and thousands of changed and transformed lives) will be forever grateful for *his faith* in me."

In the early formative stages of this new ministry, my administrative gifts were required to form a nonprofit corporation, recruit a Board of Directors, locate a usable piece of property, work with site planners and architects on a master plan, create a fundraising strategy, communicate the vision of this new camp, organize and administrate Board meetings, financials, and create a three to five-year business plan for the formation of a brand new ministry.

The formation and early operation of this new ministry were certainly administratively heavy. However, my gift of teaching full-time staff, summer staff, and campers was essential once we opened. The combination of passion (which enabled the necessary perseverance) and the use of spiritual gifts (to give both my Board, the full-time and summer staff confidence and preach effectively with both staff and campers) was essential in the formation of this new Christian camping ministry for the city of Houston, Carolina Creek Christian Camps. Campers and parents often commented to me about how "lucky" I was to be at camp. I would smile and agree, knowing internally that all "luck" in life comes with a price. And as I like to say now, **LUCK** stands for "**L**iving **U**nder **C**hrist's **K**indness."

NEED

As mentioned, after extensive market research in cooperation with Christian Camp and Conference Association (CCCA), formally Christian Camping International (CCI), Houston, Texas, was identified as one of the largest metropolitan areas in the United States underserved in the Christian camping industry. Therefore, I moved to Houston, where I was an athletic trainer, professor, and Christian school administrator. My amazing wife was a teacher, athletic director, and coach while creating the plan for a brand-new camp for the Houston area. I chose the Houston area because of the *need* based on the large population, many churches of all sizes and denominations, and the number of Christian schools to support the summer individual camper program and the off-season retreats. Many of these organizations and ministries reported having nowhere to go for camp or retreats. Houston *needed* a facility like the one we were passionate about building. And we deeply desired to impact as many people as possible spiritually. It would not have made sense for us to move to Branson, Missouri, the home of Kanakuk, one of the biggest camping organizations in the world, or, to move to Fresno, California, in the backyard of Hume Lake, another large Christian camping organization.

In other words, I selected a large metropolitan area, a demographic that had a *need* for a Christian camp that would enable me to combine my *passion* for Christian Camps with my *gifts* of administration and teaching in an area of *need* in the United States of America. Therefore, with a passionate group of Board members and donors, the faith and provision of a Board Chairman and His wife, with God's empowerment, wisdom, and direction, my wife and I formed Carolina Creek Christian Camps just north of Houston in Huntsville, Texas. This brand new ministry represented this author's **passion** (Christian camping), **spiritual gifts** (administration and teaching), and **need** (Houston, Texas, one of the largest metropolitan areas with no camp within 90 miles at that time).

After providing prayerful, persevering, and pioneering leadership to this amazing and life-transforming place of ministry for fifteen years, and believing that I would serve there for the rest of my life, with *God's direction and many reservations* (like the Lord asking Abraham to sacrifice Isaac in Genesis 22), I moved to Liberty University, the world's largest Christian University, to pursue my greatest *passion* – teaching. Specifically, *teaching God's Word* and the valuable lessons from a *lifetime of serving in Christian camping* to train, equip, and send out the next generation of Christian camping leaders. Now, as the Director of Camp and Outdoor Adventure Leadership (COAL) at Liberty University, the world's largest Christian university, I get to teach, train, and send out the next generation of Christian camping leaders ("So Christ himself gave the apostles, the prophets, the evangelists, the pastors and teachers, to equip his people for works of service, so that the body of Christ may be built up until we all reach unity in the faith and in the knowledge of the Son of God and become mature, attaining to the whole measure of the fullness of Christ. *(Ephesians 4:11-13)*.

I also have the privilege of teaching programming in ministry, discipleship, and evangelism. I get to connect our students with camps across the country, camps to other camps, consult with dozens of camps annually, and travel and teach God's Word to retreats and summer campers all over the country, not just Houston, Texas, when I am not in the classroom at Liberty. At Carolina Creek Christian

Camps and Liberty, I have followed my **passion,** utilized my **spiritual gifts**, and met a **need**. I also deeply desire for you to walk faithfully in God's vocational will for your life and incorporate these three powerful elements.

My father told me once if you do something that you enjoy, you will never work a day in your life. Well, Dad, I agree with you. And now, I would simply add for my children, my students, campers, and all people, "if you do something that you are **passionate** about, use your **spiritual gifts**, and meet the **needs** of others, you will never work a day in your life."

Enjoy your journey.
Live your purpose.
EPHESIANS 2:10

REFERENCES

Amabile, T. M., Hill, K. G., Hennessey, B. A., & Tighe, E. M. (1994). The Work Preference Inventory: Assessing intrinsic and extrinsic motivational orientations. *Journal of Personality & Social Psychology, 66*(5), 950-967.

Anderson, G. H. (1999). Biographical dictionary of Christian missions. *Missiology. 27*(1):41-45. https://doi: 10.1177/009182969902700109.

Arnett, J. J. (2000). Emerging adulthood: A theory of development from the late teens through the twenties. *American Psychologist, 55*(5), 469-480.

Astin, A.W., & Panos, R.J. (1969). *The educational and vocational development of college students.* American Council on Education.

Attride-Stirling, J. (2001). Thematic networks: An analytic tool for qualitative research. *Qualitative Research, Vol. 1*(3), 385-405.

Bandura, A. (1991). Social cognitive theory of self-regulation. *Organizational Behavior and Human Decision Processes, 50*(2), 248-287. https://doi:10.1016/0749-5978(91)90022.

Baumeister, R.F. (1991). *Meanings of life.* Guilford.

Baumeister, R. F., Wotman, S. R., & Stillwell, A. M. (1993). Unrequited love: On heartbreak, anger, guilt, scriptlessness, and humiliation. *Journal of Personality & Social Psychology, 64*(3), 377-394.

Beggs, J. M., Bantham, J. H., & Taylor, S. (2008). Distinguishing the factors influencing college students' choice of major. *College Student Journal, 42*(2), 381.

Bellah, R.N., Madsen, R., Sullivan, W.M., Swidler, S.M., & Tipton, S.M. (1986). *Habits of the heart: Individualism and commitment in American life.* Harper & Row.

Berg, J.M., Dutton, J.E., & Wrzesniewski, A. (2008). What is job crafting and why does it matter? *Ross School of Business, University of Michigan, from the Center for Positive Organizational Scholarship.*

Berg, J. M., Grant, A. M., & Johnson, V. (2010). When callings are calling: Crafting work and leisure in pursuit of unanswered occupational callings. *Organization Science, 21*(5), 973-994. https://doi:10.1287/orsc.1090.0497.

Bertram, R. M. (1996). The irrational nature of choice: A new model for advising undecided students? *NACADA Journal, 16*(2), 19-24.

Bird, P. A. (1981). "Male and female He created them": Gen 1:27b in the context of the priestly account of creation1. *Harvard Theological Review, 74*(2), 129–160.

Black, S.J., & Ashford, S.J. (1995). Fitting in or making jobs fit: Factors affecting mode of adjustment for new hires. *Human Relations, 48*(4), 421-437.

Blackaby, H., & King, C. (1994). *How to live the full adventure of knowing and doing the will of God.* Broadman and Holman Publishers.

Blackaby, H. Blackaby R., & King, C. (2008). *Experiencing God: Knowing and doing the will of God.* B & H Publishing Group.

Bolles, R. N. (2019). *What color is your parachute?* Crown Publishing Group.

Boyd, J.R. (1859). *Westminster shorter catechism: With analysis, scriptural proofs, explanatory, and practical inferences, and illustrative anecdotes.* Presbyterian Board of Publication.

Boyer, E.L. (1987). *College: The undergraduate experience in America.* Harper & Row.

Braumeister, R. F., Wotman, S. R., & Stillwell, A. M. (1993). Unrequited love: On heartbreak, anger, guilt, scriptlessness, and humiliation. *Journal of Personality & Social Psychology, 64*(3), 377-394.

Brewster, P.S. (1976). Pentecostal Doctrine. *Cheltenham, 47*(2), 95-112.

Briki, W. (2017). Passion, trait self-control, and wellbeing: Comparing two mediation models predicting wellbeing. *Frontiers in Psychology, 8.*

Bugbee, B. (2005). *What you do best in the body of Christ: Discover your spiritual gifts, personal style, and God-given passion.* Harper Collins.

Bunderson, J. S., & Thompson, J. A. (2009). The call of the wild: Zookeepers, callings, and the double-edged sword of deeply meaningful work. *Administrative Science Quarterly, 54* (1), 32-57. https://doi:10.2189/asqu.2009.54.1.32.

Campbell, D.T. & Stanley, J. (1963). Experimental and quasi-experimental designs for research. *Handbook of research on teaching.* Rand McNally.

Cardon, M. S. (2008). Is passion contagious? The transference of entrepreneurial passion to employees. *Human Resource Management Review, 18*(2).

Charmaz, K. (2006). *Constructing grounded theory.* Sage.

Clifton, D. (2007). *Strengths finder 2.0.* Gallup Press.

Colozzi, E. A., & Colozzi, L. C. (2000). College students' callings and careers: An integrated values-oriented perspective. In D. A. Luzzo (Ed.), *Career counseling of college students: An empirical guide to strategies that work* (pp. 63-91). American Psychological Association. https://doi:10.1037/10362-004.

Cooper, J.O., Heron, T.E., & Heward, W.L. (2007). *Applies behavior analysis.* Pearson/Merrill-Prentice Hall.

Creswell, J.W. & Creswell, J.D. (2018). *Research design: qualitative, quantitative, and mixed-method approaches* (5th edition). Sage.

Csikszentmihalyi, M. (1990). *Flow: The psychology of optimal experience.* Harper & Row.

Dalton, J. C. (2001). Career and calling: Finding a place for the spirit in work and community. *New Directions for Student Services, 95,* 17-25. https://doi:10.1002/ss.19.

Denscombe, M. (1998). *The good research guide: For small-scale social research projects.* Open University Press.

Diemer, M. A., & Blustein, D. L. (2007). Vocational hope and vocational identity: urban adolescents' career development. *Journal of Career Assessment, 15,* 98-118. https://doi:10.1177/1069072706294528.

Dik, B.J., Eldridge, B.M., Steger, M.F., & Duffy, R.D. (2012). Development and validation of the calling and vocational questionnaire (CVQ) and Brief Calling Scale (BCS). *Journal of Career Assessment, 20* (3), 242-263.

Dik, B.J., & Duffy, R.D. (2009). Calling and vocation at work: definitions and prospects for research and practice. *The Counseling Psychologist, 37*(3), 424-450.

Dobrow, S.R., & Tosti-Kharas, J. (2011). Calling: the develop of a scale measure. *Personnel Psychology, 64*(4), 1001-1049.

Dobrow, S. R., & Tosti-Kharas, J. (2012). Listen to your heart? Calling and receptivity to career advice. *Journal of Career Assessment, 20*(3), 264-280.
https://doi:10.1177/1069072711434412.

Dostoevsky, F. (2018). *The gambler.* Scotts CreateSpace Independent Publishing.

Dubin, R. (1956). Industrial worker's worlds: A study of the "central life interest" of industrial workers. *Social Problems, 3*(3), 131-142.

Duckworth, A. L., Peterson, C., Matthews, M. D., & Kelly, D. R. (2007). Grit: Perseverance and passion for long-term goals. *Journal of Personality and Social Psychology, 92*(6), 1087.

Duffy, R. D., Allan, B. A., Autin, K. L., & Bott, E. M. (2013). Calling and life satisfaction: It's not about having it, it's about living it. *Journal of Counseling Psychology, 60*(1), 42–52.

Duffy, R.D., & Autin, K.L. (2013). Disentangling the link between perceiving a calling and living a calling. *Journal of Counseling Psychology, 60*(2), 219-227.

Duffy, R.D., Bott, E.M., Allan, B.A., Torrey, C.L., & Dik, B.J. (2012). Perceiving a calling, living a calling, and job satisfaction: testing a moderated, multiple mediator model. *Journal of Counseling Psychology, 59*(1), 50-59.

Duffy, R.D., & Dik, B.J. (2013). Research in calling: what have we learned, and where are we going? *Journal of Vocational Behavior, Vol. 83* (3), 428-436.

Duffy, R. D., Manuel, R. S., Borges, N. J., & Bott, E. M. (2011). Calling, vocational development, and well-being: A longitudinal study of medical students. *Journal of Vocational Behavior, 79*(2), 361-366. https:// doi:10.1016/j.jvb.2011.03.023.

Dussel, E. (1978). The differentiation of charisms. *Concilium 109*(3), 38-55.
https//:gospelstudies.org.uk

Elangovan, A.R., Pinder, C.C., & McLean, M. (2010). Callings and organizational behavior. *Journal of Vocational Behavior, 76*(3), 428-440. https://psycnet.apa.org/record/2010-06921-006.

Elliot, E. (1997). *God's guidance: A slow and certain light.* Fleming H. Revell Co.

Edwards, J. (2011). God's sovereignty in the salvation of men. *https://hopeof glory.com/AFW/sas_pdf/gsitsom.pdf.*

Ferguson, S.B. (1992). *Discovering God's will.* Banner of Truth.

Fincham, J.E. (2008). Response rates and responsiveness for surveys, standards, and the journal. *American Journal of Pharmaceutical Education* 72 (2): 43.

Fetterman, D.M. (2010). *Ethnography: Step by step.* Sage

Fischer, G.W., Damodaran, N., Laskey, K.B., & Lincoln, D. (1987). Preferences for proxy attributes. *Management Science 33*(2): 198-214.

Fowler, F.J. (2008). *Survey research methods* (4th Edition). Sage

Fowler, F.J. (2014). *Survey research methods* (5th Edition). Sage

Friesen, G. L. (2004). *Decision-making and the will of God.* Multnomah.

Friesen, G.L. (1978). *God's will as it relates to decision making.* A dissertation presented to
        Dallas Theological Seminary, Dallas, TX.

Galotti, K.M., & Mark, M.C. (1994). How do high school students structure an important life decision? A short-term longitudinal study of the college decision-making process. *Research in Higher Education 35*(5): 589-607.

Getz, G. (1974). *Sharpening the focus of the church.* Moody Press.

Getz, G. (1976). *Building up one another.* Victor Books.

Gilley, P. (2002). *Home to harmony.* HarperCollins Publisher, Inc.

Grant, A.M. (2007). Relational job design and the desire to make a prosocial difference. *Academy of Management Review, 32*(2), 393-417.

Grant, A.M. (2008). The significance of task significance: Job performance effects, relational mechanisms, and boundary conditions. *The Journal of Applied Psychology 93*(1), 108-124.

Greenhaus, J. H. (1971). An investigation of the role of career salience in vocational behavior. *Journal of Vocational Behavior, 1*(3), 209-216. https://doi:10.1016/0001-8791(71)90022-4.

Grudem, W. (1993). Should Christians expect miracles today? Objections and answers from the Bible, Part 4. *Journal of Ministry Resources and Theology for Pentecostal and Charismatic Ministry & Leaders, 12*(2). http://pneumareview.com/should-christians-expect-miracles-today.

Grudem, W. (1993). Power & Truth: A response to the critiques of vineyard teaching and practice by D.A. Carson, James Montgomery, and John H. Armstrong in Power Religion. Vineyard Position Paper #4, Power & Truth, A Response to Power Religion, *The Association of Vineyard Churches.*

Grudem, W. (1994). *Systematic theology: An introduction to biblical doctrine.* Zondervan.

Guinness, O. (2003). *The call: Finding and fulfilling the central purpose of your life.* W Publishing Group.

Haas, S.B. (2012). Five steps to finding your passion: discovering what you love most is an adventure in itself. *Psychology Today, 27*(2) 24-31.

Hackman, J.R. & Oldham, G.R. (1976). Motivation through the design of work: test of a theory. *Organizational Behavior and Human Performance, 16*(2), 250-279.

Hagmaier, T., & Abele, A.E. (2012). The multidimensionality of calling: conceptualization, measurement, and a bicultural perspective. *Journal of Vocational Behavior, 81*, 39-51.

Hall, D.T., & Chandler, D.E. (2005). Psychological success: when the career is a calling. *Journal of Organizational Behavior, 26*(2), 155-176.

Hanegraaff, H. (2001). *The face that demonstrates the farce of evolution.* Word Publishing.

Hardy, L. (1990). *The fabric of this world: Inquiries into calling, career choice, and the design of human work.* William B. Eerdmans Publishing Company.

Heasley, B., & Hurford, J. (1977, 1983). *Semantics: A coursebook.* J. Lyons, Semantics (2 volumes). Cambridge Publishing.

Hernandez, E. F., Foley, P. F., & Beitin, B. K. (2011). Hearing the call: a phenomenological study of religion in career choice. *Journal of Career Development, 38*(1), 62-88. https://doi:10.1177/0894845309358889.

Hiebert, D.E. (1984). *First Peter: An expositional commentary.* Moody Press.

Hill, R.E., & Miller, E.L. (1981). Job change and the middle seasons of a man's life. *Academy of Management Journal,* 24 (1), 114-127.

Hirschi, A. (2011). Callings in career: a typological approach to essential and optional components. *Journal of Vocational Behavior, 79*(1), 60-73.

Horowitz, D. L. (2001). *The deadly riot: The calculus of passion.* Los Angeles, CA: University of California Press.

Horton, D.J. (2009). Discerning spiritual discernment: assessing current approaches for understanding God's will. *The Journal for Youth Ministry, 7* (2), 7-31.

House, H.W. (1992). The doctrinal issues in Colossians: Part 2. *Bibliotheca Sacra.* Dallas Theological Seminary Publishing.

Hu, N. B. (1996). *Effects of college students' perceptions of labor market variables and conditions on their choice of academic majors.* Association for Institutional Research Annual Forum Paper, Albuquerque, NM.

Hunt, M. (1993). *The story of psychology.* Anchor Books.
Hunter, I., Dik, B.J., & Banning, J.H. (2010). College student's perceptions of calling in work and life: a qualitative analysis. *Journal of Vocational Behavior, 76*(2), 178-186.

Hybels, B. (1990). *Honest to God: Becoming an authentic Christian.* Zondervan.

Hybels, B. (2007). *Holy discontent: Fueling the fire that ignites personal vision.* Zondervan.

Hybels, B. (2009). *Courageous leadership: Field-tested strategy for the 360-degree leader.* Zondervan.

Hybels, B., & Cordeiro, W. (2012). *The power of a whisper: Hearing God, having the guts to respond* (Reprint edition). Zondervan.

Ilgen, D.R., & Hollenbeck, J.R. (1992). The structure of work: Job design and roles. *Handbook of Industrial/Organizational Psychology*. Consulting Psychologists Press.

James, S. (1997). *Passion and action: The emotions in seventeenth-century philosophy*. Oxford University Press.

Julia Moeller. (22:20:01 UTC). *Two sides of the same coin: Are the Dual Types of Passion?* https://www.slideshare.net/JuliaMoeller1/two-sides-of-the-same-coin-are-the-dual-types-of-passion-types-in-the-sense-of-distinct-subgroups-of-individuals.

Kahn, W.A. (1990). Psychological conditions of personal engagement and disengagement at work. *Academy of Management Journal, 33*(4), 692-724.

Käsemann, E. (1969). *New testament questions of today*. Fortress Press.

Kelley, T. L. (1927). *Interpretation of educational measurements*. Macmillan.
Kilner, J.F. (2015). *Dignity and destiny: Humanity and the image of God*. Eerdmans Publishing.

King James Bible. (2017). Cambridge University Press. (Original work published 1769)

Kovach, S.D. (2000). *Toward a theology of guidance: a multi-faceted approach emphasizing scripture as both foundation and pattern in discerning the will of God*. A dissertation submitted to Trinity Evangelical Divinity School.

Kramer, G. L., Higley, H. B., & Olsen, D. (1994). Changes in academic major among undergraduate students. *College and University, 69*(2), 88-96.

Laurentin, R. (1978). Charisms: Terminological precision. *Concilium 109*(3), 9-11.

Leslie, L.L. (1972). Are high response rates essential to valid surveys? *Social Science Research, 1*(3), 323-334.

Lewis, C.S. (1996). *Mere Christianity*. Simon and Schuster.

Litten, L.H. (1982). Different strokes in the application pool: some refinements in a model of student college choice. *Journal of Higher Education 55*(4): 383-402.

Litten, L.H. (1991). *Ivy bound: High ability students and college choice*. College Board.

Locke, E. A., & Latham, G. P. (1990). *A theory of goal setting and task performance*. Prentice-Hall.

Lord, R. G., Diefendorff, J. M., Schmidt, A. M., & Hall, R. J. (2010). Self-regulation at work. *Annual Review of Psychology, 61*(3), 543-568. doi:10.1146/annurev.psych.093008.100314.

Loscocco, K.A. (1989). The interplay of personal and job characteristics in determining work commitment. *Social Science Research, 18*(4), 370-394.

Lowe. S., & Lowe, M. (2018). *Ecologies of faith in a digital age: Spiritual growth through online education*. InterVarsity Press Academic.

Lu, A., & Gursoy, D. (2016). Impact of job burnout on satisfaction and turnover intention: do generational differences matter? *Journal of Hospitality & Tourism Research. Vol.40*(2), 210-235

MacArthur, J.F. (2012). *Found: God's will.* Cook Communications Ministries.

MacArthur, J.F. (1994). *Reckless faith.* Crossway Books.

MacArthur, J. F. (2002). *Twelve ordinary men.* Thomas Nelson, Inc.

Manchiraju, S., & Sadachar, A. (2018). Passion and self-determination: exploring social networking site addiction using a dualistic framework. *Social Networking, 07*(03), 126–136.

Maslow, A.H. (1943). A theory of human motivation. *Psychological Review, 50*(4), 370-396.

Mattson, R.T., & Miller, A.F. (1999). *Finding a job you can love.* Thomas Nelson Publishers.

McCabe, K. (2018). How to write a post-event survey: With 40+ example event questions. *Learn Hub. https://learn.g2.com/how-to-write-post-event-survey.*

McLeod, S. (2018). Maslow's hierarchy of needs. *SimplyPsychology. http://www.simplypsychology.org/simplypsychology.org-Maslows-Hierarchy-of-Needs.pdf.*

McLoud, S. (2019). What is a Likert Scale? *SimplyPsychology.* https://www.simplypsychology.org/likert-scale.html.

Moeller, Julia (n.d.) *Two sides of the same coin: Are the Dual Types of Passion Types in the....* Education. https://www.slideshare.net/JuliaMoeller1/two-sides-of-the-same-coin-are-the-dual-types-of-passion-types-in-the-sense-of-distinct-subgroups-of-individuals.

Moule, C. F. D. (1953*). An idiom-book of new testament greek.* Cambridge University Press.

Nash, L. & McLennan, S. (2001). *Church on Sunday, work on Monday: The challenge of fusing Christian values with business life.* Jossey-Bass.

Nevo, B. (1985). Face validity revisited. *Journal of Educational Measurement, 22*(4), 287-293.

Ng, E., Lyons, S., & Schwelzer, L. (2010). New generation, great expectations: A field study of the millennial generation. *Journal of Business Psychology, 25*(3), 281-292.

New International Version Bible. (1983). Zondervan. (Original work published 1978)

Novak, M. (1996). *Business as a calling: Work and the examined life.* The Free Press.

Packer, J.I. (1984). *Keep in step with the Spirit.* Fleming H. Revell Co.

Packer, J.I. (1973). *Knowing God.* InterVarsity Press.

Payne, E. (2007*). God confronts culture: The almost complete biblical and Christian worldview.* Covenant Books.

Pentecost, D. (1997). *The divine comforter, the person and work of the Holy Spirit.* Kregel.

Peterson, K.F. (2006). *Changing their majors: How do students choose their majors and why do so many change?* A dissertation presented to the faculty of the University of Minnesota.

Philippe, F. L., Vallerand, R. J., & Lavigne, G. L. (2009). Passion Does Make a Difference in

People's Lives: A Look at Well-Being in Passionate and Non-Passionate Individuals. *Applied Psychology: Health and Well-Being, 1*(1), 3–22. https://doi.org/10.1111/j.1758-0854.2008.01003.x.

Pink, A. W. (2001). *The sovereignty of God.* Sovereign Grace Publishers, Inc.

Praskova, A., Creed, P. A., & Hood M. (2014). The development and initial validation of a career calling scale for emerging adults. *Journal of Career Assessment, 23*(1). https://doi:10.1177/1069072714523089.

Popper, K. (1959). *The logic of scientific discovery.* Basic Books.

Rahner, K. (1979). *The Spirit in the church.* London.

Robertson, A.T. (1934*). A grammar of the Greek New Testament in the light of historical research.* Broadman Press.

Robson, C. (1993). *Real-world research: a resource for social scientists and practioner-researchers.* Blackwell Publishers.

Roese, N.J., & Summerville, A. (2005). What we regret most...and why. *HHS Public Access, US National Library of Medicine National Institutes of Health.* https://www.ncbi.nlm.nih.gov/pmc/articles/PMC2394712/

Rohm, Robert, A. (2008). *Positive Personality Profiles.* Personality Profiles Press.

Rosso, B.D., Dekas, K.H., & Wrzesniewski, A. (2010). On the meaning of work: a theoretical integration and review. *Research in Organizational Behavior, 30*(2), 91-127.

Rudestam, K.E. & Newton, R.R. (2014). *Surviving your dissertation* (4th Edition). Sage.

Ryan R.M. & Deci, E.L. (2001). On Happiness and human potentials: a review of research on hedonic and eudemonic well-being. *Annual Review of Psychology, Vol. 52*(2), 141-166.

Schafer, J.L., & Graham, J.W. (2002). Missing data: our view of the state of the art. *Psychological Methods, 7*(2), 147-177.

Schein, E. (1978). *Career dynamics: Matching individual and organizational needs.* Addison-Wesley.

Schwarz, B. (2005). *The paradox of choice: Why more is less.* Harper Perennial.

Scott, E. (2020). *Verywellmind.* https://www.verywellmind.com/stress-and-burnout-symptoms-and-causes-3144516.

Shaw, J.D., & Gupta, N. (2004). Job complexity, performance, and well-being: when does supplies-values fit matter? *Personnel Psychology. Vol. 57*(4), 847-879.

Shields, B.J. (2008). *An assessment of dropout rates of former youth ministry participants in conservative southern baptist megachurches.* A dissertation presented to the faculty of the Southern Baptist Theological Seminary.

Shulman, S., & Nurmi, J.-E. (2010). Dynamics of goal pursuit and personality make-up among emerging adults: Typology, change over time, and adaptation. In S. Shulman & J.-E. Nurmi (Eds.), *The role of goals in navigating individual lives during emerging adulthood* (pp. 57-70). Wiley Periodicals.

Sisson, J. (1986). Jeremiah and the jerusalem conception of peace. *Journal of Biblical Literature, 105*(3), 429-442. https://doi:10.2307/3260511.

Smith, K.C. (2008). *The modified wisdom view of guidance: the normative use of scripture and God-given wisdom in decision making, with the possibility of divine special guidance.* A thesis presented to Southeastern Baptist Theological Seminary.

Smith, M. B. (1991). *Knowing God's will: Finding guidance for personal decisions.* InterVarsity Press.

Spurgeon, C. H. (1862). God's will and man's will. Sermon no. 442, delivered on Sunday morning, March 30, 1862, Metropolitan Tabernacle, Newington. *Spurgeon's Sermons, 8 (2),* 117-127.

Stake, R.E. (1995). *The art of case study research.* Sage

Stanley, A. (2010). *Discovering God's will study guide: How to know when you are heading in the right direction.* WaterBook Multnomah Publishing.

Steger, M. F., Pickering, N. K., Shin, J. Y., & Dik, B. J. (2010). Calling in work: Secular or sacred? *Journal of Career Assessment, 18*(1), 82-96. https://doi:10.1177/1069072709350905.

St. John, E. (2000). Majors. *Black Issues in Higher Education, 15*(2), 21–27.

Stringfellow, A.B. *Great characters of the Bible: 52 Lessons on how God used ordinary people to accomplish extraordinary tasks.* Whitaker House.

Sullivan, D. M. (2016). We believe in human life is fearfully and wonderfully made. *Cedarville University, Pharmacy Practice Faculty Publications, 290* (2), https://digitalcommons.cedarville.edu/cgi/viewcontent.cgi?article=1289&context=pharmacy_practice_publications.

Swindoll, C. (1999). *What does God want for me?* Thomas Nelson, Inc.

The Best Thyroid Disorders Blogs of 2017. (n.d.). *Healthline.* https://www.healthline.com/health/hypothyroidism/best-thyroid-blogs.

The Passion To Persist Download Full – PDF Book Download. (n.d.-a). https://all-med.net/pdf/the-passion-to-persist/.

Theophilides, C., Terenzini, P. T., & Lorang, W. (1984). Freshman and sophomore experiences and changes in major field. *The Review of Higher Education, 7*(3), 261-278.

Thompson, D. and Miller-Perrin, C. (2003) "Understanding Vocation: Discerning and Responding to God's Call. *Leaven 11*(1), Article 11. https://digitalcommons.pepperdine.edu/leaven/vol11/iss1/11.

Thrasher, B. (2001). *Living the life God has planned: A guide to knowing God's will.* Moody Publishers.

Tozer, A.W. (1957). How the Lord leads. *Alliance Weekly,* January 2, 1957.

Vallerand, R.J. (2007). On the Role of Passion in Performance. *Journal of Personality, 73*(3), 505-534. https://onlinelibrary.wiley.com/doi/full/10.1111/j.1467-6494.2007.00447.x

Vallerand, R. J. (2010). On passion for life activities: The dualistic model of passion. In *Advances in experimental social psychology 42*(2), 97–193.

Vallerand, R. J. (2012). From motivation to passion: In search of the motivational processes involved in a meaningful life. *Canadian Psychology/Psychologie Canadienne, 53*(1), 42.

Vallerand, RJ. (2015). *The psychology of passion: A dualistic model.* Oxford, England: Oxford University Press.

Vallerand, R. J. (2015). *The psychology of passion: A dualistic model.* Series in Positive Psychology.

Vallerand, R. J. (2016). The dualistic model of passion: Theory, research, and implications for the field of education. In *Building autonomous learners* (pp. 31–58). Springer.

Vallerand, R. J., Blanchard, C., Mageau, G. A., Koestner, R., Ratelle, C., Leonard, M., & Gagne, M. (2003). Les passions de l'Ame: On obsessive and harmonious passion. *Journal of Personality and Social Psychology, 85*(4), 756-767. https://doi:10.1037/0022-3514.85.4.756.

Vallerand, R. J., & Carbonneau, N. (2013). The role of passion in optimal functioning in society. *Theory Driving Research: New Wave Perspectives on Self-Processes and Human Development,* 53–82. https://www.researchgate.net/publication/316791646.

Vallerand, R. J., Houlfort, N., & Fores, J. (2003). Passion at work. *Emerging Perspectives on Values in Organizations, 6*(8), 175–204.

Vallerand, RJ. & Houlfort (2019). *Passion for work: Theory, research, and applications.* Oxford, New York: Oxford University Press.

Vallerand, R. J., Houlfort, N., & Forest, J. (2014). Passion for work: Determinants and outcomes. *Oxford Handbook of Work Engagement, Motivation, and Self-Determination Theory, 12*(2), 85–105.

Vallerand, R. J., Mageau, G. A., Elliot, A. J., Dumais, A., Demers, M.-A., & Rousseau, F. (2008). Passion and performance attainment in sport. *Psychology of Sport and Exercise, 9*(3), 373–392.

Vallerand, R. J., & Miquelon, P. (2007). *Passion for sport in athletes.*

Vallerand, R. J., Paquet, Y., Philippe, F. L., & Charest, J. (2010a). On the role of passion for work in burnout: A process model. *Journal of Personality, 78*(1), 289–312.

Vallerand, R. J., & Verner-Filion, J. (2013). Making people's life most worth living: on the importance of passion for positive psychology. *Terapia Psicológica, 31*(1), 35–48.

Vernon, A. (1958). *A Quaker businessman: A biography of Joseph Rowntree (1836-1925).* Allen & Unwin.

Vygotsky, L.S. (1978). *Mind in society: The development of higher psychological processes.* Harvard University Press.

Warfield, B. (1965). *Miracles: Yesterday and today, true and false.* Eerdmans Publishing Company.

Weiss, J. W., Skelley, M. F., Haughey, J. C., & Hall, D. T. (2004). Calling, new careers, and spirituality: A reflective perspective for organizational leaders and professionals. *Research in Ethical Issues in Organizations, 5*(2), 175-201. https://doi:10.1016/S1529-2096(03)05009-0.

Willard, D. (1999). *Hearing God: Developing a conversational relationship with God.* InterVarsity Press.

Wilson, McNair, C. (2012). *Hatch: Brainstorming secrets of a theme park designer.* Book Villages.

Whitney, R. Ringwald, edited by John F. Rauthmann (2021). The handbook of personality dynamics and processes. Bielefeld University Academic Press.

Wolcott, H.T. (2008). *Ethnography: A way of seeing.* AltaMira.

Wright, B. E. (2007). Public service and motivation: does mission matter? *Public Administration Review. Vol. 67*(1), 54-64.

Wrziesniewski, A. (2012). Callings. *Oxford handbook of positive organizational scholarship.* Oxford University Press.

Wrzesniewski, A., Dekas, K., & Rosso, B. (2009). Callings. In S. Lopez & A. Beauchamp, *Encyclopedia of positive psychology, 115-118.* Blackwell.

Wrziesniewski, A., and Dutton, J.E. (2001). Crafting a job: Revisioning employees as active crafters of their work. *Academy of Management Review, 26*(2)*, 179-201.*

Wrzesniewski, A., McCauley, C., Rozin, P., & Schwartz, B. (1997). Jobs, careers, and callings: People's relations to their work. *Journal of Research in Personality, 31*(1), 21-33. https://doi:10.1006/jrpe.1997.2162.

Yin, R.K. (2009). *Case study research: Design and methods* (4th Edition). Sage.

Yin, R.K. (2012). *Applications of case study research* (3rd Edition). Sage

Made in United States
Orlando, FL
31 May 2024

47359601R10153